# THE
# AMERICAN
# COOKBOOK

# THE AMERICAN COOKBOOK

## A fresh take on classic recipes

ELENA ROSEMOND-HOERR
CAROLINE BRETHERTON

LONDON NEW YORK MUNICH
MELBOURNE DELHI

**Senior Editor** Bob Bridle
**Senior Art Editor** Lucy Parissi
**Editorial Assistant** Elizabeth Clinton
**Managing Editor** Dawn Henderson
**Managing Art Editor** Christine Keilty
**US Editor and Consultant** Rebecca Warren
**US Editorial Director** Nancy Ellwood
**Senior Jacket Creative** Nicola Powling
**Jacket Design Assistant** Rosie Levine
**Senior Pre-Production Producer** Tony Phipps
**Senior Producer** Oliver Jeffreys
**Art Director** Peter Luff
**Publisher** Peggy Vance

DK INDIA
**Senior Editor** Dorothy Kikon
**Senior Art Editor** Balwant Singh
**Editor** Arani Sinha
**Art Editor** Simran Kaur
**Assistant Editor** Aditi Batra
**Assistant Art Editor** Pooja Verma
**Managing Editor** Alicia Ingty
**Managing Art Editor** Navidita Thapa
**Production Manager** Pankaj Sharma
**Pre-Production Manager** Sunil Sharma
**DTP Designers** Rajesh Singh Adhikari,
Rajdeep Singh Rawat

**Studio photography** Stuart West
**Additional photography** Elena Rosemond-Hoerr

First American edition, 2014

Published in the United States by
DK Publishing, 4th Floor, 345 Hudson Street,
New York, NY 10014

A Penguin Random House Company

14 15 16 17 18  10 9 8 7 6 5 4 3 2 1
001–197059–Feb 2014

Copyright © 2014 Dorling Kindersley Limited

A catalog record for this book is available from the
Library of Congress.

ISBN 978-1-4654-1587-5

DK books are available at special discounts when
purchased in bulk for sales promotions, premiums,
fundraising, or educational use. For details, contact:
DK Publishing Special Markets, 345 Hudson Street,
New York, NY 10014 or SpecialSales@dk.com.

Printed and bound in China by South China Printing
Co. Ltd

Discover more at
**www.dk.com**

# CONTENTS

# INTRODUCTION

America's cuisine is as varied and diverse as its residents, with each region boasting a unique, culinary heritage that has been passed down from generation to generation. "Manifest Destiny"—a 19th-century belief that settlers were destined to spread across the continent—created an environment in which immigrants from around the world shared stories and traded recipes. So Jewish peddlers introduced fried green tomatoes to the Southeast after the Civil War, Italian immigrants stewed pots of cioppino on the wharf of San Francisco, African Americans fried chicken and waffles in Brooklyn after the Great Migration, and Lebanese immigrants mixed up hummus and tabbouleh in Detroit. These are just some of the shared traditions that are deeply embedded in the American relationship with food.

As a Southerner with family ties to Ireland, Scotland, England, Sicily, Poland, and who knows where else, I blend techniques and ingredients from all over the world in my North Carolina kitchen. On my grits I pile homemade sauerkraut (a nod to my husband's Pennsylvania Dutch heritage), pico de gallo, chorizo, and Vermont sharp Cheddar cheese; and you are as likely to see shrimp and sweet potato quesadillas topped with an avocado cream on our dinner table as you are chicken pot pie with Cheddar chipotle biscuits.

In this sense, I am a typical American, able to draw inspiration from the world's cuisines and present them with a twist—a new take on an old favorite. This book does just that, celebrating the best that America has to offer in a fresh and inspiring way, truly capturing the country's rich, diverse, and ever-evolving food culture.

**Elena Rosemond-Hoerr**

# STARTERS, SOUPS, AND SALADS

# GRILLED PEACH SALSA WITH CORN CHIPS

Full of vibrant colors and flavors, this salsa is great by itself or as an accompaniment to grilled fish.

★ **SERVES** 4
★ **PREP TIME** 20 mins, plus chilling
★ **COOK TIME** 15 mins

### Ingredients

2 large peaches, not too ripe, halved and pitted
1 tbsp olive oil
2 ripe tomatoes, skinned, seeded, and finely chopped
1 large green onion, trimmed and finely chopped
½ jalapeño or other mild green chile, seeded and finely chopped
2 tbsp finely chopped cilantro
2 tbsp finely chopped mint
1 tbsp extra virgin olive oil
1 tbsp lime juice
1 tsp hot sauce
salt and freshly ground black pepper

### For the corn chips

8 x 6in (15cm) corn tortillas
1 tbsp olive oil, or some olive oil spray
4 tsp spice mix, such as Old Bay or Cajun spice, or smoked paprika

**1** Heat a grill pan or a barbecue grill to high heat. Grill the peach halves for 2–3 minutes on each side, until they blacken in places and start to soften. Cool, peel, and finely dice the peaches.

**2** Transfer the peaches to a medium bowl and add the remaining salsa ingredients. Season to taste. Chill the salsa in the fridge for 1 hour to allow the flavors to develop.

**3** Preheat the oven to 450°F (230°C). Brush or spray the corn tortillas on both sides with a little oil, then sprinkle ½ tsp spice mix on each. Pile the spiced tortillas in a stack, then cut them into 6 equal wedges. Lay out the spicy wedges in a single layer on several baking sheets, taking care that they do not touch each other.

**4** Bake in the oven for 5 minutes, checking them after 3 minutes, as they can burn easily. They should be brown and crispy in places, but still chewy in the middle. Remove from the oven and place onto a wire rack to cool and crisp up further. Serve with the peach salsa, brought to room temperature before serving.

**COOK'S TIP** Many oils and fats are now available in spray form. While many are artificial, and should be avoided, a natural olive oil spray is ideal here for coating the tortillas with a thin, even layer of oil.

# CHUNKY GUACAMOLE FETA SALSA

More substantial than a guacamole dip, this salsa is perfect with grilled lamb or beef.

★ **SERVES** 4
★ **PREP TIME** 10 mins
★ **COOK TIME** 15 mins

### Ingredients

1 corn cob
1 tbsp olive oil
2 ripe avocados, halved, pitted, and cut (see technique, below)
12 cherry tomatoes, halved or quartered, if large
2 large scallions, trimmed and finely chopped
2 heaped tbsp chopped cilantro
juice of 1 lime
1 tsp hot sauce
salt and freshly ground black pepper
½ cup feta cheese

**1** Rub the corn cob with oil and grill for 5–10 minutes, turning occasionally, until lightly charred in places. Alternatively, grill it on a grill pan over high heat, or roast it directly over a gas flame or on a barbecue grill. Set it aside to cool.

**2** When cool enough to handle, rest it vertically on a chopping board and, with a sharp knife, cut downward to shear off the kernels (see technique, p152).

**3** In a large bowl, place the corn, avocados, tomatoes, and all but 1 tbsp each of the scallions and cilantro. Toss them together with the lime juice and hot sauce, and season well.

**4** Place the guacamole in a large bowl and crumble over the feta cheese. To serve, top with the remaining green onions and cilantro.

## STONING AND PEELING AN AVOCADO

**1 Slice the avocado** lengthwise in half, cutting all the way around the central pit, then separate the two halves by twisting gently.

**2 Strike the pit** with the blade of a large knife to embed it, then twist and lift the knife to remove the stone.

**3 Cut each avocado half** in half again. Use a paring knife to lift off the skin gently. Cut into ½in (1cm) chunks to use in the recipe.

# BUFFALO CHICKEN WINGS

Hailing from Buffalo, New York, these sweet, spicy wings are served with a salty blue cheese dressing.

- ★ **SERVES** 6
- ★ **PREP TIME** 20-30 mins, plus resting
- ★ **COOK TIME** 40-50 mins

## Ingredients

1 cup all-purpose flour
1 cup breadcrumbs
1 tsp paprika
½ tsp cayenne pepper
½ tsp salt
2 cups buttermilk (or to make your own, see Cook's tip, right)
24 bone-in chicken wings
1¾ pints (1 liter) peanut or sunflower oil, for frying
1 cup hot sauce
2 garlic cloves, chopped
2 tbsp honey
1 stick butter

## For the cheese dressing

2 tbsp mayonnaise
½ cup sour cream
¼ cup buttermilk
½ cup blue cheese, crumbled
2 tbsp apple cider vinegar

**1** In a large bowl, combine the flour, breadcrumbs, paprika, cayenne pepper, and salt. Pour the buttermilk into a separate bowl. Dip the chicken wings in the buttermilk and toss them in the flour mixture, coating each one evenly. Refrigerate the coated chicken wings for at least 1 hour.

**2** In a large, heavy-based saucepan or deep-fat fryer, heat the oil to 375°F (190°C), as shown in the technique on p144.

**3** Meanwhile, in another saucepan, combine the hot sauce, garlic, honey, and butter and place over low heat. Let the butter melt, then simmer for 5 minutes.

**4** When the oil is hot, fry the chicken pieces in batches, 4–5 pieces in each batch, for 8–10 minutes, or until golden brown. Remove the fried pieces from the oil with a slotted spoon and dip them in the sauce mixture. Turn the pieces through the mixture to coat them on all sides. Place on a wire rack to cool.

**5** For the blue cheese dressing, process the mayonnaise, sour cream, buttermilk, blue cheese, and vinegar in a food processor. Serve the dressing in a small bowl alongside the chicken.

**COOK'S TIP** If buttermilk isn't available, you can make your own buttermilk substitute by combining 1 tbsp of lemon juice or vinegar with 1 cup of lowfat milk. Let it stand for 10 minutes before using.

## NOW TRY...

### HONEY & CHIPOTLE

For a honey chipotle glaze, combine
¾ cup **honey**, 2 tbsp **hot sauce**, and
1 tbsp **chipotle paste**.

### RANCH DRESSING DIP

Mix ¼ cup **mayonnaise**, ¼ cup
**buttermilk**, ½ cup **sour cream**,
½ tsp each of **onion powder**, freshly
ground black pepper, **garlic powder**,
and **dried thyme**, and
1 tbsp chopped **parsley**.

### BAKED WINGS

For a sweet and salty baked variation, add
½ cup crushed **sweet potato crisps** to
the breading and bake on a parchment
paper-lined rack at 400°F (200°C) for
40 minutes, glazing with the sauce
mixture every 10 minutes.

# SMOKY BACON POTATO SKINS

Loaded with delicious fillings, these stuffed potato skins would make a welcome addition to any Super Bowl party.

★ **MAKES** 12
★ **PREP TIME** 20 mins
★ **COOK TIME** 1 hr 20 mins

### Ingredients

6 baking potatoes, about
  2¾in (7cm) long, scrubbed
1 tbsp peanut or sunflower oil,
  plus extra for brushing
3 smoked bacon slices
3 tbsp sour cream
1 tsp smoked paprika or ancho
  chile powder
salt and freshly ground
  black pepper
¾ cup finely grated cheese,
  such as sharp Cheddar
2 green onions, trimmed and
  finely chopped
sour cream, to serve
snipped chives, to serve

**1** Preheat the oven to 400°F (200°C). Put the potatoes in a bowl and drizzle over 1 tbsp of oil. Rub the potatoes all over with the oil, then pierce them with a fork and set them on a baking sheet. Bake for about 45 minutes, turning once, until they are cooked through and golden brown. Set aside to cool.

**2** Meanwhile, put the bacon on a baking sheet and cook in the oven for about 10 minutes, turning once, until crispy. Drain on paper towels and set aside to cool, then dice it very finely.

**3** Turn the oven up to 450°F (230°C). When the potatoes are cool enough to handle, cut them horizontally in half. Scoop out the insides, leaving a small amount of potato attached to the skin to make a sturdy shell. Brush the potato shells all over with a little oil, then put them back on the baking sheet, skin-side up. Bake them for 10 minutes, then turn them over and bake for a further 5 minutes. Remove from the oven.

**4** While the shells are crisping, place the scooped-out cooked potatoes in a bowl, add the sour cream and smoked paprika, and season well. Mash until smooth.

**5** Set aside a little of the grated cheese and add the rest to the mashed potato mixture, along with the chopped crispy bacon and the green onions. Mix well and stuff the filling into the crisped shells, mounding it up slightly in the center.

**6** Top the loaded potato skins with the remaining cheese and bake for a further 10 minutes, until they are golden brown and hot right through. Serve with a teaspoon of sour cream and a sprinkling of snipped chives, if desired.

**COOK'S TIP** Cook the potatoes up to 3 days in advance—when using the oven for another dish perhaps—and chill them until needed.

**Green onions** add bite to the rich filling and cook quickly, too.

# SPICY CHICKEN NACHOS WITH JALAPEÑOS

## Tender shredded chicken makes a healthy alternative to the more traditional pulled pork.

★ **SERVES** 4
★ **PREP TIME** 30 mins
★ **COOK TIME** 25–30 mins

### Ingredients

6oz (175g) skinless boneless
    chicken breast
salt and freshly ground
    black pepper
pinch of chile flakes
1 x 8oz bag tortilla chips
1 x 15oz can black beans,
    drained

**For the pico de gallo**

2 red tomatoes, seeded
    and diced
1 red onion, diced
handful of cilantro, chopped,
    plus extra for garnishing
juice of 1 lime

**For the quick pickles**

1 red onion, thinly sliced
1 jalapeño or other mild green
    chile, cut into ¼in (5mm) slices
1 cup apple cider vinegar
1 tsp sea salt

**For the queso**

½ cup half-and-half
1 cup grated Pepper Jack
    cheese or mozzarella
olive oil
1 onion, diced
2 garlic cloves, crushed
1 jalapeño or other mild green
    chile, finely chopped

**1** For the pico de gallo, mix the tomatoes and onion with the cilantro and lime juice. Season to taste and set aside.

**2** For the quick pickles, combine the onion and jalapeño in a nonreactive saucepan (not aluminum or cast iron) with the vinegar and sea salt and cook over low heat. Simmer for 5 minutes until the jalapeño turns dark green and the onion is translucent. Remove from the heat and set aside.

**3** For the queso, put the cream and cheese in a small heatproof bowl over a saucepan of simmering water, making sure the bowl does not touch the water. Cook for 10 minutes, stirring occasionally as the cheese melts.

**4** Meanwhile, heat some oil in a small pan over medium heat and sauté the onion and garlic. Add the jalapeño. Once the jalapeño has softened slightly and the onion is translucent, stir in the melted cheese. Reduce the heat and stir occasionally.

**5** Sprinkle the chicken with salt, pepper, and chile flakes and grill for 5–6 minutes on each side. Let it cool slightly, then shred with a fork.

**6** Lay out half of the tortilla chips on a large plate, then pour over half the queso, followed by the black beans. Add a second layer of chips and the remaining queso. Top with the chicken, pico de gallo, and drained pickles. Garnish with cilantro before serving.

**COOK'S TIP** If time is short, try using store-bought salsa and thinly sliced red onions for a quick but tasty alternative to the pico de gallo and the quick pickles.

# TROPICAL TEXAS CAVIAR

This healthy, zesty dish is equally delicious as a simple dip with tortilla chips, or served alongside grilled meat or fish.

★ **SERVES** 4–6

★ **PREP TIME** 15 mins, plus resting

**Ingredients**

1 jalapeño or other mild green chile, seeded and finely chopped

1 mango, peeled and roughly chopped

½ pineapple or 7oz (200g) canned pineapple, cut into cubes

2 garlic cloves, crushed

1 red bell pepper, seeded and roughly chopped

1 green bell pepper, seeded and roughly chopped

1 red onion, roughly chopped

1 tomato, roughly chopped

12oz (340g) can corn, drained

15oz (400g) can black-eyed peas, drained

juice of 4 limes

salt and freshly ground black pepper

tortilla chips, to serve

**1** In a large bowl, mix the jalapeño, mango, pineapple, garlic, peppers, onion, and tomato. Combine well with the corn and black-eyed peas.

**2** Add the lime juice, season well, and cover. Leave to rest for 1 hour to allow the flavors to develop.

**3** Serve chilled or at room temperature with tortilla chips for dipping.

### WHAT'S THE STORY?

Texas caviar is a cold dish of cooked black-eyed peas soaked in vinaigrette and enhanced with various chopped vegetables and herbs. Black-eyed peas are a heat-loving plant widely grown in Texas, where Helen Corbett, a chef and cookbook writer who advocated the use of fresh ingredients, popularized the dish in the 1950s.

**Mangoes**, with their vivid color and sweet flavor, contrast well with many savory salads.

# DEVILED DUCK EGGS WITH SMOKED SALMON

Adding lemon, dill, and smoked salmon can turn a simple boiled egg into an indulgent starter, picnic dish, or sandwich filling.

★ **MAKES** 8 egg halves
★ **PREP TIME** 15 mins, plus cooling
★ **COOK TIME** 15 mins

**Ingredients**
4 duck eggs
1 heaped tbsp sour cream
1 tbsp chopped dill, plus extra to garnish
1 tbsp chopped chives
grated zest of ½ lemon
1 tsp lemon juice
salt and freshly ground black pepper
1oz (30g) smoked salmon, finely diced

**1** Place the eggs in a medium, heavy-based saucepan and cover with cold water. Bring the water to a boil, then reduce to a simmer and cook the eggs for 15 minutes until hard-boiled. Remove the pan from the heat, rinse the eggs under cold running water, and leave them to cool.

**2** When the eggs are cold, peel off the shells, cut them in half horizontally and, using a teaspoon, carefully scoop out the egg yolks into a small bowl, leaving the egg whites intact. Cover the egg whites with plastic wrap and chill until needed.

**3** Mash the egg yolks well with the back of a fork. Add the rest of the ingredients, except the smoked salmon, and mash them together until smooth. Season to taste.

**4** Pile the filling into the center of the reserved egg whites with a spoon. Alternatively, transfer the filling into a piping bag and pipe into each egg half. Top with the diced salmon and garnish with dill.

**Duck eggs** have a rich flavor and an attractive dark yellow yolk.

# PIGS IN BLANKETS WITH PARMESAN PASTRY

These simple appetizers are a family favorite and can be made with whatever sausages you prefer.

★ **MAKES** 12
★ **PREP TIME** 30 mins, plus chilling
★ **COOK TIME** 25–30 mins

**Ingredients**

1 cup all-purpose flour, plus extra for dusting
½ tsp paprika
½ tsp salt
freshly ground black pepper
8 tbsp unsalted butter, chilled
¼ cup finely grated Parmesan cheese
12 cocktail sausages
1 tbsp Dijon mustard
1 egg, beaten, for glazing
ketchup and hot sauce, or a crème fraîche and mustard dip, to serve

**1** Sift the flour, paprika, salt, and a good grinding of pepper into a large mixing bowl. Coarsely grate the chilled butter directly into the flour mixture (dipping the butter in the flour first will stop it from sticking to the grater). Add the Parmesan cheese and mix well so that the butter is evenly distributed throughout the flour.

**2** Make a well in the center of the flour mixture and add 3–4 tbsp of ice water. Bring the mixture together to form a rough dough, wrap in plastic wrap, and chill for 30 minutes.

**3** Preheat the oven to 400°F (200°C). On a lightly floured surface, roll out the dough to a 12 x 10in (30 x 25cm) rectangle. Cut the rectangle into 12 strips, each measuring ¾ x 12in (2 x 30cm). If you do not get 12 strips, bring the trimmings together, re-roll, and cut until you have the required number of strips.

**4** Brush the surface of the sausages with a little of the Dijon mustard, then wrap the pastry strips around the sausages in a spiral fashion, overlapping the pastry slightly and pressing lightly at each end to seal it. The ends of the sausages may stick out of the pastry. Lay the finished sausages on an oven sheet. Brush them lightly with a little egg wash and bake for 25–30 minutes, until golden brown.

**5** Leave to cool on a wire rack for at least 5 minutes before serving hot, warm, or at room temperature. A little ketchup mixed with hot sauce, or a crème fraîche and mustard dip would be an ideal accompaniment to these savory snacks.

# FRIED SHRIMP WITH LEMON AÏOLI

Japanese panko breadcrumbs give these shrimp a real crunch. Day-old breadcrumbs work well, too.

★ **SERVES** 4
★ **PREP TIME** 10 mins
★ **COOK TIME** 12-16 mins

### Ingredients
2 cups peanut or sunflower
    oil, for frying
1 egg
1 cup all-purpose flour
1 tsp paprika
½ tsp cayenne pepper
½ tsp salt
1 cup panko breadcrumbs
    or day-old breadcrumbs
24 shrimp, peeled and
    deveined

### For the lemon aïoli
½ cup mayonnaise
juice of ½ lemon
3 scallions, chopped
2 garlic cloves, crushed
salt and freshly ground
    black pepper

**1** In a large, heavy-based saucepan or deep-fat fryer, heat the oil to 375°F (190°C), as shown in the technique on p144.

**2** Break the egg into a bowl, add 1 tbsp water, and whisk with a fork. In a separate large bowl, mix the flour, paprika, cayenne pepper, salt, and breadcrumbs.

**3** Dip the shrimp in the egg wash and toss them in the breadcrumb mixture, coating each one evenly. Fry the shrimp in batches of 6 for 3–4 minutes each, or until golden brown.

**4** For the aïoli, whisk the mayonnaise, lemon juice, onions, and garlic in a small bowl and season to taste. Serve with the shrimp.

**COOK'S TIP** When deep-frying, make sure you do not overcrowd the pan as the shrimp will not brown well.

**Shrimp** come in all shapes and sizes, but look for wild-caught shrimp if possible.

# NOW TRY...

## HOT & SPICY SAUCE

Mix together ½ cup **mayonnaise**, 2 tbsp **hot sauce**, 1 tbsp **soy sauce**, and 1 tsp **red chile paste**. Toss the shrimp in the sauce and serve with toothpicks.

## ASIAN-STYLE DIP

Combine 2 tbsp **honey**, 2 tbsp **soy sauce**, and ½ tbsp **ground ginger** for an Asian-style dipping sauce.

## BAKED OPTION

For a lighter alternative to frying, add ¼ cup grated **Parmesan** to the breading and bake the coated shrimp at 450°F (230°C) for 5-7 minutes, or until golden brown, turning once so they are evenly browned.

# LEMON SHALLOT CRAB CAKES

Fresh crabs, fished from the Chesapeake Bay, are traditionally used to make these famous Maryland crab cakes.

★ **MAKES** 4
★ **PREP TIME** 15 mins
★ **COOK TIME** 6–10 mins

### Ingredients

10oz (300g) cooked white and
   brown crabmeat (to extract
   crabmeat from shell, see p25)
1 egg
²/₃ cup crushed crackers or dried
   breadcrumbs
juice of 1 lemon, plus extra
   to serve
zest of 2 lemons
salt and freshly ground
   black pepper
1 shallot, finely chopped
2 garlic cloves, crushed
peanut or sunflower oil,
   for frying

### For the aïoli

1 cup mayonnaise
juice of 1 lemon
bunch of scallions,
   finely chopped
1 garlic clove, crushed

**1** Rinse and pick over the crabmeat, removing any pieces of shell, then drain well. In a bowl, mix together the crab, egg, crackers, lemon juice and zest, and season to taste. Add the shallot and garlic, and mix well.

**2** Take a quarter of the mixture and form a cake 3in (7.5cm) in diameter and set aside on a plate. Repeat to make 3 more cakes.

**3** Pour the oil into a large, heavy-based frying pan to a depth of at least 1in (2.5cm). Heat the oil to 375°F (190°C), and fry the cakes for 3–5 minutes on each side, or until golden.

**4** Meanwhile, make the aïoli. Mix together the mayonnaise, lemon juice, scallions, and garlic in a bowl. Season to taste. Serve the crab cakes hot with the aïoli and a squeeze of lemon.

**COOK'S TIP** Add a finely chopped jalapeño or other mild green chile to step 1 for a spicy twist.

**Lemon**, freshly squeezed, adds a bright tartness to the rich flavor of seafood.

# NEW ENGLAND CRAB DIP

Adding Greek yogurt to the mayonnaise gives a light, fresh taste to this dip, enhanced here with lemon and herbs.

★ **SERVES** 6

★ **PREP TIME** 5 mins

**Ingredients**

1lb (450g) white crabmeat, cooked or canned (drained)

4 tbsp thick Greek yogurt

2 tbsp good-quality mayonnaise

1 tbsp finely chopped dill

1 tbsp finely chopped chives

finely grated zest of ½ lemon

¼ tsp cayenne pepper

salt and freshly ground black pepper

crackers or homemade baguette bruschetta, to serve

**1** If using crabmeat from a cooked crab, extract the white meat, as shown in the technique below. Place the crabmeat in a bowl and mash it finely with the back of a fork to break up any large pieces.

**2** Whisk together the yogurt and mayonnaise until well combined, then fold it into the crabmeat.

**3** Add the dill, chives, lemon zest, and cayenne pepper and mix well. Season to taste. Serve with crackers or homemade baguette bruschetta (see Warm artichoke and spinach dip, p26).

## EXTRACTING MEAT FROM A COOKED CRAB

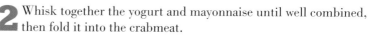

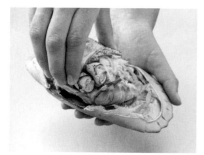

**1 Twist off the claws** and legs and set them aside. Twist off the tail flap and discard. Break and separate the body from the shell. Discard the gills and stomach sac.

**2 Cut the body** into quarters and pick out the white meat with a fork. Using a nut cracker, break the shell of the claws and the legs across their narrowest part, and extract the white meat.

**3 Using a spoon**, scoop out the white meat from the shell. Remove and reserve the brown meat for another time and discard any pieces of shell or membrane from the crabmeat.

# SPICY CORN FRITTERS WITH SALSA

If you're using young, tender corn, there is no need to cook it before making these flavor-loaded fritters.

★ **SERVES** 4
★ **PREP TIME** 20 mins
★ **COOK TIME** 10 mins

**Ingredients**

2 corn cobs, about
   9oz (250g) kernel weight
¾ cup self-rising flour
1 tsp baking powder
2 large eggs
4 tbsp milk
1 tsp smoked paprika
   or ancho-chilli powder
2 scallions, finely chopped,
   green and white parts
   separated
4 tbsp chopped cilantro
1 red chile, seeded and
   finely chopped (optional)
salt and freshly ground
   black pepper
2 tbsp peanut or sunflower oil
2 ripe tomatoes, skinned and
   roughly chopped
2 tbsp extra virgin olive oil
dash of Tabasco or chili sauce

**1** Hold the corn cobs upright on a chopping board and, using a sharp knife, cut downward to shear off the kernels (see technique, p152).

**2** Sift the flour and baking powder into a bowl. Mix the eggs and milk together in a bowl and gradually whisk them into the flour to make a thick batter. Add the corn, paprika, the white parts of the scallions, 2 tablespoons of the cilantro, and the chile (if using). Mix well and season.

**3** Heat the peanut or sunflower oil in a large frying pan and add tablespoonfuls of the batter mixture. Use the back of the spoon to spread the fritters out slightly, and fry for 2–3 minutes on each side until puffed up and golden brown. Fry in batches until all the mixture is cooked, adding a little more oil as necessary.

**4** Put the tomatoes, the remaining cilantro and scallions, olive oil, and Tabasco or chili sauce into a food processor and process until blended but still quite chunky. Check the salsa for seasoning and serve the hot fritters with the salsa on the side.

# WARM ARTICHOKE AND SPINACH DIP

This rich, creamy dip is delicious served warm with home-made bruschetta or simple sliced baguette.

- ★ **SERVES** 4-6
- ★ **PREP TIME** 15 mins
- ★ **COOK TIME** 30 mins, plus cooling

### Ingredients

1 day-old baguette, thinly sliced

1 tbsp olive oil, plus extra for brushing

2 tbsp unsalted butter

2 garlic cloves, crushed

¾ cup baby spinach

¾ cup artichoke hearts preserved in oil, drained weight

1 cup cream cheese

½ cup finely grated Parmesan cheese

½ cup sour cream

1 tbsp all-purpose flour

¾ cup grated Gruyère cheese

freshly ground black pepper

**1** Preheat the oven to 350°F (180°C). Spread out the slices of baguette in a single layer over 1 or 2 baking sheets and brush them on both sides with a little oil. Bake them in the top of the oven for about 5 minutes on each side, until they are golden brown and crispy. Set aside to cool.

**2** Melt the butter and oil in a large saucepan over medium heat. Add the garlic and cook for 2 minutes, until golden. Add the spinach and continue to cook for 2–3 minutes, stirring constantly, until the spinach wilts. Place the spinach in a sieve and press down with the back of a spoon to remove any excess liquid. Let it cool, then roughly chop it.

**3** Rinse the artichokes under cold running water and pat them dry. Roughly chop them and set them aside. Place the cream cheese, Parmesan, sour cream, flour, and half of the Gruyère cheese in a food processor and process until smooth.

**4** Add the spinach and artichokes to the mixture, season with pepper, and pulse briefly until the mixture is well combined, but with small chunks of vegetables still visible.

**5** Pour the mixture into individual ramekins or a 8in (20cm) ovenproof baking dish. Scatter with the remaining Gruyère cheese and bake at the top of the oven for 25–30 minutes, until the top is golden brown and the cheese is bubbling on the sides. Allow to cool for 10 minutes before serving with the baked baguette bruschetta.

**Artichokes,** even when canned or frozen, add a rich, luxurious taste to this dip.

# NOW TRY...

## MIDDLE EASTERN DIP

For a Middle Eastern twist, add ½ tsp each of ground **cumin** and **coriander** to the cheese, and serve with **tortillas** brushed with olive oil, scattered with **sesame seeds**, and baked in a hot oven until crispy.

## SAUTÉED KALE

Spinach can be easily replaced with **sautéed kale**, which has a stronger flavor, although it will need to be cooked for 1 or 2 minutes longer.

## GREEK YOGURT

For a simple, fresh dip, omit the Gruyère cheese, replace the sour cream with an equal amount of **Greek yogurt**, and serve without baking.

# SPICY PIMIENTO CHEESE DIP

This versatile dip can be processed smooth as a dip for crackers or potato chips, or coarse for a sandwich filling.

★ **SERVES** 6

★ **PREP TIME** 10 mins, plus chilling

**Ingredients**

2¼ cups grated sharp cheddar cheese
¼ cup sour cream
¼ cup good-quality mayonnaise
¼ cup finely diced roasted red peppers (pimientos), from a can or jar
2 large scallions, trimmed and finely chopped
1 tsp smoked paprika
1 tsp cayenne pepper
salt and freshly ground black pepper, to taste
crackers or homemade baguette bruschetta, to serve

**1** Put all the ingredients into a food processor and pulse until the mixture is well combined, but rough in texture.

**2** Place the mixture in an airtight container and chill for at least 1 hour to allow the flavors to develop.

**3** Serve with crackers or homemade baguette bruschetta (see Warm artichoke and spinach dip, p26).

**COOK'S TIP** This tasty dip makes a delicious alternative filling for a Grilled cheese sandwich (see p90), layered with crispy, grilled prosciutto or applewood smoked bacon.

## SERVE WITH

**BUFFALO CHICKEN WINGS**
SEE PAGE 12

**CHEDDAR CHEESE STRAWS**
SEE PAGE 230

# ASIAN CHICKEN AND RICE NOODLE SOUP

## Make this with homemade chicken stock to get a second delicious meal from a simple roasted chicken.

★ **SERVES** 4
★ **PREP TIME** 20 mins
★ **COOK TIME** 25 mins

### Ingredients

2 tbsp olive oil
2 stalks of lemongrass, trimmed
bunch of scallions, trimmed and
   roughly chopped
2 red chiles, seeded
   and halved
2in (5cm) piece of ginger,
   cut into slices
small bunch of cilantro,
   leaves and stalks separated
5 cups hot chicken stock
7oz (200g) cooked
   chicken, shredded
1 cup soup noodles,
   such as vermicelli
salt and freshly ground
   black pepper

**1** Heat the oil in a large saucepan. Roughly bruise the lemongrass with a rolling pin. Add the lemongrass, scallions, chiles, ginger, and cilantro stalks to the saucepan and cook over medium heat for 2 minutes to release their flavors.

**2** Add the stock and bring to a boil. Reduce the heat to a gentle simmer and cook for about 20 minutes, until the vegetables are soft. Take the saucepan off the heat and pass the stock through a sieve to remove the vegetables. Wipe the saucepan clean and return the flavored stock to the heat.

**3** Add the chicken and noodles, and continue to cook until the noodles are ready (according to the package instructions). Check the seasoning. Roughly chop the cilantro leaves and scatter over the hot soup before serving immediately.

**COOK'S TIP** If you have extra stock, double the quantities and cook up to step 3. Add the chicken, but leave out the noodles. Freeze it in portions. Then, when needed, defrost the portions, bring to a boil, add the noodles, and cook until tender.

### WHAT'S THE STORY?

Chicken noodle soup is a deeply comforting soup traditionally made from the long, slow simmering of a whole chicken. Although versions of this soup appear in several cuisines worldwide, the Jewish kitchens of America's East Coast have a special claim. The soup has attained the almost mythical (yet unproven) status as a cure for the common cold, among other ailments.

# TORTILLA CHICKEN SOUP

Full of the vibrant flavors of the Southwest, this colorful, hearty soup is a meal in itself.

★ **SERVES** 6
★ **PREP TIME** 20 mins
★ **COOK TIME** 45 mins

### Ingredients

3 tbsp olive oil
2 garlic cloves, crushed
1 jalapeño or other mild green chile, finely chopped
1 red onion, diced
1 green bell pepper, seeded and roughly chopped
1 red bell pepper, seeded and roughly chopped
15oz (400g) can corn, drained
15oz (400g) can black beans, drained
3 tbsp cornmeal or grits
2 x 15oz (400g) can chopped tomatoes
salt and freshly ground black pepper
2 tsp chipotle paste
5 cups hot chicken stock
2 chicken breasts, 12oz (350g) in total

### To garnish

3 tortillas, cut into ½in (1cm) strips
handful of cilantro, chopped
½ cup grated Cheddar cheese
juice of 1 lime

**1** Heat 1 tbsp of the oil in a large soup pot over medium heat. Add the garlic, jalapeño, and onion, and cook over medium heat for 3–4 minutes. Add the peppers with the corn, beans, and cornmeal. Simmer, stirring occasionally, for 2–3 minutes.

**2** Stir in the tomatoes with their juices, a little salt, 1 tsp of the chipotle paste, and the stock. Reduce the heat to low and simmer for 35 minutes.

**3** Meanwhile, season the chicken on both sides with salt and black pepper, and smear all over with the remaining chipotle paste. Heat 1 tbsp of the oil in a frying pan and cook the chicken breasts for 8–10 minutes per side, then cut them into ½in (1cm) slices and add to the soup.

**4** Heat the remaining oil in a large frying pan over low-medium heat. Sauté the tortilla strips for 2–3 minutes, or until crisp and browned. Serve the soup hot, garnished with the cilantro, cheese, lime juice, and tortilla strips.

**Chipotle chiles**, common in Mexican cuisine, are smoke-dried jalapeños.

# SPICY CHORIZO MINESTRONE

A classic Italian minestrone is given added spice with the use of chorizo, a Spanish cured pork sausage.

★ **SERVES** 8–10
★ **PREP TIME** 20 mins
★ **COOK TIME** 2 hrs

**Ingredients**

1 tbsp olive oil
3 garlic cloves, crushed
9oz (250g) red onion, chopped
8oz (225g) green bell pepper,
   seeded and chopped
9oz (250g) celery stalks, chopped
7oz (200g) carrots, sliced
8oz (225g) zucchini, roughly
   chopped, skin-on
2 x 14oz (400g) can chopped
   tomatoes
14oz (400g) can chickpeas
3 cups hot chicken stock
8oz (225g) cherry tomatoes
salt and freshly ground
   black pepper
1lb 5oz (600g) chorizo
1 cup Parmesan rind
2oz (60g) kale, de-ribbed
   and chopped
8oz (225g) dried orecchiette
   pasta
6oz (175g) Portobello
   mushrooms, sliced

**1** Heat the oil in a large soup pot over medium heat and add the garlic. Stir in the onion, pepper, celery, carrots, and zucchini. Cook for 5 minutes. Add the chopped tomatoes, chickpeas with their juices, stock, and cherry tomatoes. Season and bring to a boil.

**2** Remove the skin from the chorizo and crumble the sausage meat into a frying pan. Cook for 5–7 minutes, until browned. Reserve the drippings and transfer the chorizo to the soup pot, along with the Parmesan. Stir to incorporate, reduce the heat, and simmer, uncovered, for 1 hour 45 minutes.

**3** Stir in the kale and pasta. Cook for a further 15–20 minutes, or until the pasta is tender.

**4** Meanwhile, cook the Portobello mushrooms in the frying pan with the chorizo drippings over medium heat for 3–5 minutes, until browned. Season to taste. Serve the soup hot, topped with the Portobello slices.

**Carrots** are loaded with vitamins, and make a good addition to almost any soup or stew.

# CREAMY TOMATO SOUP WITH CORN AND PEPPERS

This delicate soup brings together the best of the summer's vegetable harvest in one creamy bowlful.

★ **SERVES** 8
★ **PREP TIME** 20 mins
★ **COOK TIME** 1½ hrs

**Ingredients**

3 tbsp olive oil
2 garlic cloves, crushed
1 onion, chopped
salt and freshly ground
   black pepper
⅔ cup tomato paste
4 x 14oz (400g) can chopped
   tomatoes
1 red bell pepper, seeded
   and diced
12oz (340g) can corn, drained
1¼ cup heavy cream
crusty bread or a Grilled cheese
   sandwich (see p90), to serve

**1** In a large soup pot, heat 1 tbsp of oil over medium heat. Add the garlic and onion, and season. Add the tomato paste and stir for 2–3 minutes.

**2** Add 2 cups of water, the tomatoes, and salt. Cover and simmer for 45 minutes.

**3** Toss the pepper in the remaining oil. Broil on very low heat for 3–4 minutes, or until the pepper has roasted.

**4** Using a hand-held blender, purée the tomato mixture in the pot. Stir in the corn and pepper, reserving a little of both to garnish, then add the cream. Simmer, uncovered, for a further 30–45 minutes. Remove from the heat, garnish with the reserved corn and pepper, and serve hot with crusty bread or a Grilled cheese sandwich.

**COOK'S TIP** In high summer, use the kernels from 2 fresh corn cobs instead of using canned.

# NEW ENGLAND CLAM CHOWDER

Once plentiful on the New England coast, clams were widely used as a source of cheap protein.

- ★ **SERVES** 4
- ★ **PREP TIME** 15 mins
- ★ **COOK TIME** 1 hr

### Ingredients

12oz (350g) thick-cut
  bacon, chopped
3 garlic cloves, crushed
1 large onion, roughly
  chopped
3 tbsp all-purpose flour
1 celery stalk, sliced
1lb 2oz (500g) fingerling
  potatoes, cut into thirds
1¾ pints (1 liter) hot
  chicken stock
2 x 10½ oz (300g) can
  clams
1 cup heavy cream
juice of 1 lemon
salt and freshly ground
  black pepper
flat-leaf parsley, to garnish
crusty bread, to serve

**1** In a large, heavy-based pan or soup pot, cook the bacon for 3–5 minutes, until sizzling and softened. Add the garlic, onion, flour, and celery. Cook until the onions are translucent.

**2** Add the potatoes, along with the stock, clams, and cream. Simmer for 50–60 minutes, or until the potatoes are soft.

**3** Add the lemon juice and season to taste. Garnish with the parsley and serve hot with crusty bread.

**Clams** should be treated in the same way as mussels—any left unopened after cooking should be discarded.

# NOW TRY...

## CORN CHOWDER

For a vegetarian version, use **vegetable stock** instead of chicken; substitute the bacon with 7oz (200g) **button mushrooms**, halved; and swap the clams for 12oz (340g) can **corn**.

## FRESH SEAFOOD

Make this an authentic seafood soup with 8oz (225g) **fresh clams**, 1lb (450g) **lobster tail**, and 12 cooked **jumbo shrimp**. Add for the last 10 minutes of cooking in step 2, with the lid on and slightly open.

## REDUCED FAT MILK

For a lighter soup, try substituting the cream with **reduced fat milk** or **rice milk** and blending with a food processor to incorporate.

# SMOKY SPLIT PEA SOUP

The croutons and crispy bacon garnish add a satisfying crunch to this hearty, warming soup.

★ **SERVES** 6–8
★ **PREP TIME** 5 mins
★ **COOK TIME** 1 hr 10 mins

### Ingredients

10 smoked bacon slices
1 onion, roughly chopped
2 garlic cloves, roughly chopped
2 carrots, thickly sliced
2 potatoes, quartered
3 celery stalks, chopped
1 tbsp chopped rosemary
1 tbsp chopped thyme
1 tbsp chopped oregano
8 cups hot chicken stock
1lb (450g) dry split peas
salt and freshly ground black
   pepper

### For the croutons

2 tbsp olive oil
2 garlic cloves, crushed
2–3 slices of day-old bread,
   cut into cubes

**1** Brown the bacon in a heavy-based soup pot or flameproof casserole over medium heat. Take out a small amount of bacon and set aside for garnishing.

**2** Add the onion and garlic to the pot. Stir in the carrots along with the potatoes, celery, and the herbs. Cook over low heat until the onions turn translucent, then add the stock and peas. Cover and cook over low heat for 45 minutes to 1 hour, or until the peas are soft.

**3** Transfer the mixture to a food processor or use a hand-held blender and blend to a smooth purée. Season to taste.

**4** For the croutons, heat the oil in a small pan over medium-high heat. Add the garlic and the bread and toss until brown. Crumble or finely chop the reserved bacon. Serve the soup hot, topped with the croutons and crumbled bacon.

# BLACK BEAN AND CHIPOTLE SOUP

Black beans are a good source of protein and fiber, and this soup makes a healthy and satisfying lunch in itself.

★ **SERVES** 4

★ **PREP TIME** 15 mins

★ **COOK TIME** 2–3 hrs

### Ingredients

9oz (250g) bacon, chopped
3 garlic cloves, crushed
1 onion, diced
2 x 14oz (400g) can black
   beans, unsalted
6oz (175g) cherry tomatoes,
   halved
3 cups hot chicken stock
1 tbsp ground cumin
½ tsp chipotle paste
salt and freshly ground
   black pepper

### For the topping

2 smoked bacon slices
4 tbsp sour cream
1 avocado, halved,
   pitted, and sliced
   (see technique, p11)
bunch of cilantro leaves,
   roughly chopped

**1** Put the bacon, garlic, and onion in a large soup pot and place over medium heat. Cook, stirring frequently, until the bacon begins to fry and the onions begin to soften.

**2** Stir in the beans with their juices, tomatoes, chicken stock, ground cumin, and chipotle paste. Season to taste and bring to a boil. Reduce the heat and simmer, uncovered, for 2–3 hours, or until the soup has thickened and reduced by half.

**3** In a frying pan, dry-fry the bacon slices until crisp. Remove from the pan and leave to cool, then crumble them into pieces.

**4** Serve the soup hot, topped with the bacon, a dollop of sour cream, avocado, and cilantro.

# CAESAR SALAD WITH SEARED SALMON

This salad uses an easy version of the classic Caesar dressing, replacing the traditional recipe made with raw egg.

★ **SERVES** 4
★ **PREP TIME** 20 mins
★ **COOK TIME** 20 mins

## Ingredients

2 salmon fillets, each
  5½oz (150g)
1 tbsp olive oil
salt and freshly ground
  black pepper
peanut or sunflower oil,
  for frying
3 heaped tbsp capers,
  drained and rinsed
1 large romaine lettuce,
  leaves torn
2 avocados, halved,
  pitted, and sliced
  (see technique, p11)

## For the dressing

½ cup extra virgin olive oil
1 tbsp Dijon mustard
3 tbsp good-quality mayonnaise
4 anchovy fillets, chopped
½ tsp Worcestershire sauce
1 garlic clove, crushed
2 tbsp finely grated
  Parmesan cheese
pinch of sugar

**1** Put a grill pan on high heat, or preheat the broiler on its highest setting. Rub the salmon with the olive oil, season well, and either grill in the grill pan or broil under the hot broiler for 3–4 minutes on each side. Set aside to cool, then flake the salmon into large pieces using your hands.

**2** Pour the peanut or sunflower oil into a small, heavy-based saucepan to a depth of ½in (1cm) and heat over high heat. Meanwhile, dry the capers well on a piece of paper towel. When the oil is hot, drop the capers in (be careful, they will spit) and fry for a minute until puffed up and crispy. Remove from the oil with a slotted spoon and leave to cool on clean paper towels.

**3** To make the dressing, put all the ingredients into the bowl of a mini food processor, or into a suitable container for a hand-held blender, and process or blend until the mixture has emulsified into a thick, creamy dressing. Season with pepper.

**4** To serve, put the lettuce leaves in a large bowl and toss them in the dressing. Carefully toss through the sliced avocados, then arrange the flaked salmon over the top of the salad and scatter over the deep-fried capers.

**Avocados** are packed with monounsaturated fats, which are essential for a healthy diet.

# A taste of the
# NORTHEAST

The cuisine of this corner of the United States reflects both its cultural heritage as the landing point for the early British and European settlers, as well as its varied and fertile geography.

Despite harsh winters and an inhospitable coastline, the Northeast has long been a place of plenty. For hundreds of years, the Native Americans tapped the maple tree—a local mainstay—for its sweet, sticky sap, which they boiled down to make syrup. This soon became a widespread practice among the early farmers, who also made good use of the region's fertile soils, growing the beans and squash favored by the Native Americans, as well as their own European imports. Hunters soon learned how best to capture the area's indigenous wild turkeys, and fishermen flocked to the waters around Cape Cod to fish the abundant seas. Although less bountiful than they once were, the shorelines of New England are still a rich source of oysters, clams, and lobsters.

**In New York City, global immigrants have added to the vast array of foodstuffs available, from the layered sandwiches of the Jewish delis, to the spicy delights of Chinatown.**

## FOODS AND FLAVORS

★ Chesapeake Bay, Maryland, is renowned for its **blue crabs**, as well as for seafood of all kinds. **Crab cakes** (see p22) are just one of the area's famous dishes.

★ **New England clam chowder** (see p34) marries rich **cream** from the dairy farms of Vermont with the simply prepared fresh **clams** caught off the coast.

★ **Boston baked beans** (see p146), created by the early settlers, is an interpretation of a Native American dish. Traditionally cooked on a Saturday and kept overnight in a brick oven, the beans would stay warm until the following morning, allowing the settlers to enjoy them while still adhering to strict Sabbath rules.

★ A typical **Thanksgiving dinner** in New England will include **succotash**, a mixed corn and bean dish traditionally made by the Native Americans. There are many vibrant, modern variations of the recipe (see p145).

The Reuben is the archetypal New York deli sandwich, packed with tasty fillings.

Sweet, sour, and crunchy, the Waldorf salad originated in New York and is popular the world over.

Maryland crab cakes are traditionally made using the fabulous fresh crabs of the region.

Fresh clams are often used in chowder, but canned ones, or smoked fish, are also good.

Chinatown, in New York City, offers a vast array of succulent fresh seafood.

Camden Harbour is one of the many places in Maine that produces outstanding seafood.

Best when small and sweet, the lobsters of the Eastern seaboard, sometimes known as Maine lobsters, are a regional delicacy.

# WALDORF SALAD

Created at the Waldorf Astoria Hotel in New York, this salad has been a favorite for over 100 years.

★ **SERVES** 4

★ **PREP TIME** 15 mins

**Ingredients**

2 large apples

4 celery stalks, thinly sliced

25 red seedless grapes, halved

2 tbsp toasted and crushed walnuts

¼ cup mayonnaise

juice of 1 lemon

salt and freshly ground black pepper

2 hearts of romaine lettuce

**1** Remove the cores of the apples by using a corer. Then, using a sharp knife, cut the apples into slices of an even thickness. Stack the slices, a few at a time, and cut lengthwise through the pile and then crosswise, making equal-sized cubes.

**2** Put the apples, celery, grapes, and walnuts in a bowl. Add the mayonnaise and lemon juice and toss well to combine. Season to taste.

**3** Roughly chop the lettuce and divide between 4 plates. Serve the fruit and nut mixture on each bed of lettuce with a squeeze of lemon.

**Red apples**, with their bright color and crisp texture, make a great addition to any salad.

## NOW TRY...

## FRUIT & PECANS

Instead of using apples, celery, grapes, and walnuts, try combining 2 **pears**, 1½ cups **blackberries**, and ¼ cup **toasted pecans**.

## GREEK YOGURT

For a lighter take on this salad, simply substitute the mayonnaise with an equal amount of **Greek yogurt**.

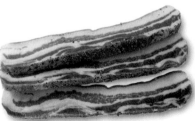

## SMOKY BACON

Add **maple-cured smoked bacon bits** for a sweet and smoky flavor. Dry-fry 8 **candied bacon crumbles** in a frying pan until crisp. Remove and allow to cool, then break them up into bits and mix into the salad.

# FRIED CHICKEN COBB SALAD

This main course salad is served with a sharp, salty buttermilk and blue cheese dressing.

★ **SERVES** 4

★ **PREP TIME** 20 mins, plus soaking

★ **COOK TIME** 20 mins

**Ingredients**

2 skinless boneless chicken breasts
1 tsp cayenne pepper
salt
1 cup whole milk
8 smoked bacon slices
½ cup all-purpose flour
½ cup breadcrumbs
1 tbsp chipotle paste
1¾ pints (1 liter) peanut or sunflower oil, for frying
bunch of baby spinach or arugula leaves
10oz (300g) cherry tomatoes, halved
1 avocado, pitted, peeled, and chopped (see technique, p11)
4 hard-boiled eggs, roughly chopped

**For the blue cheese dressing**

2 tbsp mayonnaise
½ cup sour cream
⅓ cup buttermilk (to make your own, see p12)
1 cup blue cheese, crumbled
2 tbsp apple cider vinegar

**1** Put the chicken in a pan along with the cayenne pepper and 1 tsp salt. Pour in the milk and leave the chicken to soak for 2 hours in the fridge.

**2** In a frying pan, dry-fry the bacon over medium heat until crispy. Remove from the pan and cool on a wire rack, then set aside.

**3** In a shallow bowl, mix together the flour, breadcrumbs, chipotle paste, and 1 tbsp salt. Drain and discard the milk and turn the chicken in the bread mixture until well coated.

**4** Pour the oil into a large, heavy-based saucepan or deep-fat fryer. Heat it to 375°F (190°C), as shown in the technique on p144. Fry the chicken for 5–7 minutes, or until golden brown. Remove with a slotted spoon and cool on a wire rack. Set aside.

**5** Spread the spinach evenly in a large, wide serving dish. Place the tomatoes in a row across the greens. Add the avocado, placing it next to the tomatoes, then add a row of the eggs. Chop the chicken into bite-sized pieces and distribute evenly around the salad. Crumble the bacon and scatter it over the top of the dish.

**6** For the dressing, mix together the mayonnaise, sour cream, buttermilk, blue cheese, and vinegar. Serve the salad, while the chicken is still warm, with the buttermilk dressing on the side. Any leftover dressing will keep in the fridge for up to 3 days, tightly sealed.

★ ★ ★
**WHAT'S THE STORY?**
It is widely accepted that the first Cobb salad was made at The Brown Derby restaurant in Hollywood in the early 20th century, and was named in honor of the then owner, Bob Cobb. Exactly who created it, and when, is less clear, but there is no doubt that the eponymous salad, with its distinctive stripes of fresh, colorful ingredients, is a true Tinseltown classic.
★ ★ ★

# EGG SALAD WITH CELERY, CAPERS, AND DILL

A step up from traditional egg salad, try this spread on whole-grain bread for a quick, delicious lunch.

★ **SERVES** 2-3
★ **PREP TIME** 10 mins, plus cooling
★ **COOK TIME** 10 mins

### Ingredients

6 eggs
1/3 cup good-quality mayonnaise
1 tbsp lemon juice
1 celery stalk, finely chopped
1 heaped tbsp finely chopped dill
1 heaped tbsp Dijon mustard
1 large scallion, finely chopped
1 heaped tbsp capers, drained and roughly chopped
pinch of salt and freshly ground black pepper
pinch of smoked paprika, to serve

**1** Bring a saucepan of water to a boil, lower the eggs into the water using a large spoon, and boil for 8 minutes. Remove with a slotted spoon, run under cold water, and leave to cool. When cool enough to handle, peel the shells from the eggs.

**2** In a large bowl, beat the remaining ingredients, except the paprika, until well combined.

**3** Finely chop the boiled eggs and gently mix them into the mayonnaise mixture, being careful not to break up the eggs too much. Serve sprinkled with paprika.

**COOK'S TIP** Try using this as a filling for a light, flavorsome packed lunch for children. It also serves as a good source of protein.

**Smoked paprika**, known in Spain as pimentón, has a dark, smoky spiciness that is hard to beat.

# SHRIMP, CORN, AND AVOCADO SALAD

This healthy main course salad is packed with color and flavor. Try it with baby spinach or finely shredded raw kale.

★ **SERVES** 2

★ **PREP TIME** 15 mins, plus marinating

★ **COOK TIME** 20 mins, plus cooling

### Ingredients

1 large ear of corn
7oz (200g) raw shrimp, peeled and deveined
⅓ cup finely chopped cilantro
juice of 1 lime
3 tbsp extra virgin olive oil
2 tbsp pumpkin seeds
1 tbsp Thai sweet chili sauce
salt and freshly ground black pepper
mixed salad leaves, about 3½oz (100g)
12 cherry tomatoes, halved
1 avocado, halved, pitted, peeled, and thickly sliced (see technique, p11)

**1** Heat a grill pan on high heat. Rub the corn with a little oil and grill it in the pan for 5–10 minutes, turning occasionally, until it is blackened in places and the kernels are tender. Set it aside. When it is cool enough to handle, cut the kernels off the cob with a sharp knife, as shown in the technique on p152.

**2** Meanwhile, put the shrimp in a small, nonreactive bowl (not aluminum or cast-iron), along with 1 tbsp each of the cilantro, lime juice, and oil and toss well to combine. Chill for 30 minutes.

**3** Heat a heavy-based frying pan over medium heat and add the pumpkin seeds. Toast them for 2–3 minutes, stirring frequently, until they begin to color and make a popping sound. Set aside to cool.

**4** For the dressing, put the sweet chili sauce and the remaining cilantro, lime juice, and oil in a blender or food processor. Season well and blend until it has emulsified to a thick, vivid green dressing.

**5** Reheat the grill to high heat and grill the marinated shrimp for a minute or two on each side until pink all over and charred in places. Set aside to cool.

**6** When everything has cooled down, assemble the salad. Put the mixed leaves into a bowl and toss with the dressing. Add the cherry tomatoes and corn kernels, and toss again. Arrange the avocado slices and grilled shrimp on the top, and scatter with the toasted pumpkin seeds to serve.

**Corn** is best eaten very fresh—milky kernels are a sign of freshness.

# SALAD DRESSINGS

From a rich and herby Green Goddess to a light and elegant raspberry walnut vinaigrette, these dressings enhance any salad.

### Green Goddess

★ **MAKES** 2 cups
★ **PREP TIME** 10 mins

3 anchovies from a can,
   or 2 tsp anchovy paste
2 garlic cloves, crushed
½ cup mayonnaise
½ cup sour cream
½ cup chopped parsley
¼ cup chopped tarragon
3 tbsp chopped chives
juice of 1 lemon
salt and freshly ground
   black pepper

**Put all the ingredients** in a food processor and blend until smooth. Season to taste.

### Thousand Island

★ **MAKES** 2 cups
★ **PREP TIME** 10 mins

½ cup mayonnaise
2 tbsp ketchup
2 tbsp pickle relish (see
   Spicy chow chow, p246)
2 tsp finely chopped red onion
salt and freshly ground
   black pepper

**Put all the ingredients** in a food processor and blend until smooth. Season to taste.

### Buttermilk ranch

★ **MAKES** 2 cups
★ **PREP TIME** 10 mins

4 cups mayonnaise
⅓ cup buttermilk
½ cup sour cream
½ tsp onion powder
½ tsp freshly ground
   black pepper
½ tsp garlic powder
½ tsp dried thyme
1 tbsp chopped parsley

**Put all the ingredients** in a food processor and blend until smooth. Season to taste.

### Raspberry walnut

★ **MAKES** 2 cups
★ **PREP TIME** 10 mins

½ tsp honey mustard
1 tsp sugar
¼ cup red wine vinegar
5–7 raspberries
1 shallot, about 2oz (60g)
½ cup walnut oil
salt and freshly ground
   black pepper

**Put the mustard**, sugar, vinegar, raspberries, and shallot in a food processor and pulse to a purée. Blend on a high setting, while pouring the oil in a thin stream through the opening (in the top) of the processor, until light and fluffy. Season to taste.

### Catalina

★ **MAKES** 2 cups
★ **PREP TIME** 10 mins

1 large onion, about
   12oz (350g), chopped
3 tbsp ketchup
1 tbsp sugar
2 tbsp light brown sugar
¼ cup red wine vinegar
1 tsp Worcestershire sauce
1 tsp smoked paprika or
   ancho chile powder
½ cup light olive oil or
   vegetable oil
salt and freshly ground
   black pepper

**Put the onion**, ketchup, both the sugars, vinegar, Worcestershire sauce, and smoked paprika in a food processor. Blend on a high setting, while pouring the oil in a thin stream through the opening (in the top) of the processor, until light and fluffy. Season to taste.

# HOME-STYLE POTATO SALAD

There are many ways to prepare a potato salad, and this tasty version is a Midwestern classic.

- ★ **SERVES** 6
- ★ **PREP TIME** 10 mins
- ★ **COOK TIME** 20–25 mins, plus cooling

### Ingredients

2¼lb (1kg) potatoes, peeled
salt and freshly ground
  black pepper
¼ cup good-quality
  mayonnaise
2 tsp Dijon mustard
1 celery stalk, finely
  chopped
bunch of scallions, white
  and pale green parts
  only, finely chopped
1 tbsp capers, drained
  or rinsed, and finely
  chopped
1 tbsp lemon juice

**1** Cook the potatoes whole in a large pan of boiling salted water for 20–25 minutes until tender. Drain and set aside to cool. When cold, peel and cut the potatoes carefully into 1¼in (3cm) cubes.

**2** In a bowl, mix together the mayonnaise, mustard, celery, scallions, capers, and lemon juice, and season well.

**3** Place the potatoes into a large serving bowl and gently toss the mayonnaise mixture through the potatoes, being careful not to break them up.

**Celery**, with its strong, fresh flavor, brightens up a simple potato salad.

## NOW TRY...

### FRENCH STYLE

Try making a warm new potato salad in the French style by tossing 2¼lb (1kg) still-warm **new potatoes**, halved, in a **vinaigrette**, along with a bunch of finely chopped **scallions**.

### SWEET POTATO

Substitute the potatoes for the same amount of **sweet potatoes** for an interesting variation. Cook as per the main recipe. However, they will need a shorter cooking time (around 10 minutes) and should be used while still slightly undercooked.

### EGG & BACON

Adding 2 roughly chopped hard-boiled **eggs** and 6 slices of chopped, cooked **bacon** will turn this side dish into a star attraction.

# BREAKFASTS
# AND LIGHT BITES

# WAFFLES WITH BACON MAPLE SAUCE

These easy-to-make and versatile cornmeal waffles are perfect for breakfast, a light snack, or dessert.

★ **MAKES** 6–8
★ **PREP TIME** 5 mins
★ **COOK TIME** 20–25 mins

**Ingredients**

1 cup all-purpose flour
⅓ cup fine cornmeal
   or polenta
1 tsp baking powder
2 tbsp sugar
1¼ cups milk
5 tbsp unsalted butter, melted
1 tsp vanilla extract
2 large eggs, separated
4 smoked bacon slices
½ cup good-quality
   maple syrup
jam, fresh fruit, sweetened
   cream, or ice cream,
   to serve (optional)

**1** Place the flour, cornmeal, baking powder, and sugar in a bowl. Make a well in the center and pour in the milk, butter, vanilla extract, and egg yolks. Gradually whisk together.

**2** Preheat the waffle maker or iron. In a clean, large bowl, whisk the egg whites until soft peaks form. Fold into the batter with a metal spoon.

**3** Preheat the oven to 250°F (130°C). Pour a small ladleful of the batter onto the waffle maker or iron and spread almost to the edge. Close the lid and bake until golden. Keep warm in a single layer in the oven while you make the rest of the waffles.

**4** In a frying pan, dry-fry the bacon until crispy. When cool enough to handle, crumble the bacon. Gently heat the maple syrup in a small, heavy-based saucepan over low heat. Add the bacon to the warm syrup before pouring over the waffles. Serve immediately with jam, fresh fruit, sweetened cream, or ice cream, if desired.

**COOK'S TIP** Although best eaten as fresh as possible, you can make waffles 24 hours in advance and reheat them in a toaster.

**Maple syrup**, when pure, has a strong, dark, almost smoky sweetness.

# STRAWBERRY-STUFFED FRENCH TOAST

French toast is always a treat, but this cream cheese and strawberry version would be the pride of any brunch table.

★ **MAKES** 4
★ **PREP TIME** 10 mins
★ **COOK TIME** 30 mins

**Ingredients**

8 tbsp cream cheese
8 slices of challah bread
  or brioche, each
  1½in (4cm) thick
8-12 strawberries, hulled
  and thickly sliced
4 eggs
½ cup light brown sugar
½ cup milk
1 tsp vanilla extract
1 tsp ground cinnamon
4 tbsp butter
honey, to serve

**1** Preheat the oven to 375°F (190°C). Spread 1 tbsp of the cream cheese over each slice of bread. Top 4 bread slices with 2–3 strawberries each, then cover with the remaining bread slices to make 4 sandwiches.

**2** In a bowl, whisk together the eggs, sugar, milk, vanilla extract, and cinnamon with a hand whisk. Dip the sandwiches in the egg mixture, submerging them completely.

**3** In a frying pan, melt 1 tbsp of butter over medium heat. Pan-fry the sandwiches for 3–4 minutes on each side, or until golden brown. Add the remaining butter to the pan, as needed, while frying the remaining sandwiches. Transfer to a baking sheet and put the sandwiches in the preheated oven for 5 minutes. Serve hot, drizzled with honey.

## PREPARING STRAWBERRIES

**1 To prepare a strawberry**, hold the fruit on its side on a chopping board. Using a sharp knife, cut off the stalk without removing too much fruit.

**2 Cut the strawberry** in half. Lay each half cut-side down, then cut into slices of even thickness. Repeat for the remaining strawberries.

# BUTTERMILK PANCAKES

You can make these pancakes with whole milk, but using tangy buttermilk makes them lighter.

- ★ **MAKES** 10
- ★ **PREP TIME** 5 mins
- ★ **COOK TIME** 20 mins

**Ingredients**

2 cups self-rising flour
¼ cup sugar
1 tsp baking powder
1 cup buttermilk (or to
 make your own, see p12)
2 eggs
4 tbsp unsalted butter,
 melted and cooled,
 plus extra for frying
 and serving
3-4 tbsp milk (optional)
maple syrup, to serve
fresh berries or diced fruit,
 to serve

**1** Put the flour, sugar, and baking powder into a large bowl and mix well with a balloon whisk. In a separate bowl, whisk together the buttermilk, eggs, and melted butter. Make a well in the center of the flour mixture and gradually whisk in the buttermilk mixture to a smooth, thick batter. If the batter is not quite a thick pouring consistency, stir in 3–4 tbsp milk.

**2** In a 6in (15cm) nonstick frying pan, heat a pat (about ½ tbsp) of butter over medium heat until the butter begins to sizzle. Pour in just enough batter to coat the base of the pan.

**3** Cook the pancake over medium heat until the edges are set and small bubbles appear on the surface of the pancake, burst, and leave small "holes."

**4** Turn the pancake and cook for 1–2 minutes on the other side. Serve immediately, or keep warm in a low oven while you cook the remaining pancakes. Serve with unsalted butter, maple syrup, and a bowl of fresh berries or diced fruit for an indulgent weekend breakfast treat.

## NOW TRY...

# CINNAMON & BANANA

Add 1 tsp of **ground cinnamon** to the flour. Once you have poured the batter into the pan, thinly slice half a **banana** and arrange it on top of the pancake, then cook as directed in the main recipe.

# BLUEBERRY COMPOTE

For the ultimate blueberry pancakes, make a thick compote to serve alongside. Cook down ¾ cup of ripe **blueberries** with 2 tbsp **water** and 1 tbsp **sugar** for 5 minutes, or until they burst.

# SOUTHERN TWIST

For a Southern-inspired variation, replace 1 cup of the self-rising flour with **fine polenta or cornmeal**.

# BISCUITS AND CREAMY SAUSAGE GRAVY

Traditionally served with a thick, milk-based gravy, using cream here makes this Southern favorite rich yet light.

★ **SERVES** 4
★ **PREP TIME** 15 mins
★ **COOK TIME** 20 mins

### Ingredients

2 cups self-rising flour, plus extra for dusting
1 tsp baking powder
1 tsp smoked paprika or ancho chile powder
½ tsp salt
6 tbsp unsalted butter, chilled
¾ cup coarsely grated sharp cheese
freshly ground black pepper
1 cup buttermilk (or to make your own, see p12)
1 egg, beaten with 1 tbsp cold water

### For the sausage gravy

1 tbsp peanut or sunflower oil, for frying
about 9oz (250g) spicy gourmet sausages
1 tbsp all-purpose flour
1 cup hot good-quality chicken stock
½ cup half-and-half cream

**1** Preheat the oven to 450°F (230°C). Sift the flour, baking powder, smoked paprika, and salt into a food processor. Add the butter and process until the mixture resembles fine breadcrumbs. Add the grated cheese and a good grinding of pepper, and pulse briefly to combine. Put the mixture into a large bowl and add the buttermilk. Stir with a wooden spoon, until the mixture is soft and sticky.

**2** Turn the mixture out onto a lightly floured surface and gently pat the mixture into a smooth block, then gently pat or lightly roll it out to a thickness of 1¼in (3cm). Cut rounds out of the mixture with a 2½in (6cm) biscuit cutter and place them on a baking sheet. Gather the trimmings and gently squeeze them together. Pat it out again, or re-roll, and continue to cut out more rounds until all the dough is used up.

**3** Brush the tops of the biscuits lightly with a little of the egg wash. Bake in the preheated oven for 10–12 minutes, until risen and golden brown. Remove the biscuits from the oven and allow them to rest on the baking sheet for 5 minutes before transferring them to a wire rack to cool completely.

**4** Meanwhile, make the gravy. Heat the oil in a heavy-based frying pan. De-skin the sausages and crumble the meat into the pan. Fry over high heat for 3–5 minutes, turning frequently, until the meat is brown and crispy. Reduce the heat and sprinkle the flour over the sausage. Stir, then add the stock, a little at a time, stirring constantly. Finally, add the half-and-half and reduce the heat to a low simmer. Cook for 5 minutes until the sauce has thickened. Pour it over the biscuits to serve.

# GRANOLA WITH DRIED FRUIT COMPOTE

Making your own granola is a cost-effective way of ensuring that your cereal contains exactly what you like.

★ **SERVES** 4–6
★ **PREP TIME** 10–15 mins
★ **COOK TIME** 45 mins, plus cooling

### Ingredients

¾ cup rolled oats
⅓ cup mixed seeds, such as sunflower, sesame, pumpkin, and golden linseed
½ cup mixed unsalted nuts, such as cashews, almonds, hazelnuts, and walnuts
1 tbsp light olive oil, plus extra for greasing
2 tbsp honey
¼ cup maple syrup
scant 1oz (25g) dried blueberries
scant 1oz (25g) dried cranberries
scant 1oz (25g) dried cherries
¼ cup shredded coconut
Greek yogurt or milk, to serve

### For the compote

3½oz (100g) dried apples
3½oz (100g) dried figs
3½oz (100g) dried prunes
1 cinnamon stick
½ vanilla pod, halved lengthwise
finely grated zest and juice of 1 orange
1 tbsp demerara sugar

**1** Preheat the oven to 300°F (150°C). Place the oats, seeds, and nuts in a large mixing bowl. Add the oil, honey, and maple syrup and stir well to combine.

**2** Put the mixture into a large, lightly oiled roasting pan and spread out into an even layer. Bake for 15 minutes. Mix together the berries, cherries, and coconut. Stir into the pan and bake for a further 15 minutes. Leave in the pan to cool completely. When cool enough to handle, break the granola into small pieces and transfer to an airtight container.

**3** For the compote, place all the dried fruits in a mixing bowl. Add the cinnamon, vanilla pod, and orange zest and juice. Pour in ¾ cup of boiling water. Cover the bowl and set aside overnight.

**4** Transfer the contents of the bowl to a saucepan. Add the sugar and ⅔ cup of cold water and bring to a boil. Reduce the heat and simmer very gently, uncovered, for 15 minutes. Remove the vanilla pod and cinnamon stick.

**5** Put the granola into individual bowls, pour over the compote, and serve with Greek yogurt or milk.

**COOK'S TIP** Any combination of dried fruit works well—try using apricots, peaches, or dates, or a mixture of dried berries. For a warming winter compote, add 2 finely chopped pieces of preserved ginger in syrup, plus 2 tbsp of the syrup.

# SOUTHERN-STYLE BREAKFAST CASSEROLE

A classic American brunch dish, but a relative newcomer to European tables, this is quick to assemble, and delicious.

★ **SERVES** 4-6

★ **PREP TIME** 15 mins, plus resting

★ **COOK TIME** 40 mins

**Ingredients**

1 tbsp olive oil

7oz (200g) spicy pork sausage meat

butter, for greasing

3½oz (100g) stale baguette or other coarse white bread, crusts removed and cut into ½in (1cm) cubes

4 scallions, finely sliced

1 large ripe tomato, skinned, seeded, and chopped

1 jalapeño or other mild green chile, seeded and finely chopped

⅔ cup grated sharp cheese, such as cheddar

6 eggs

½ cup half-and-half

½ cup whole milk

1 tsp smoked paprika or ancho chili powder

salt and freshly ground black pepper

**1** Heat the oil in a nonstick frying pan. Add the sausage meat to the pan and cook, chopping it up with a spatula, turning it over, and stirring until it is broken into large lumps and is well browned on all sides. Remove the pan from the heat.

**2** Preheat the oven to 350°F (180°C). Grease a 10in (25cm) flameproof casserole with the butter. Spread out the bread in a single layer in the dish, then evenly scatter over the sausage meat. Sprinkle over the scallions, tomato, and jalapeño, then top with the cheese.

**3** In a bowl, lightly beat together the eggs, half-and-half, milk, and smoked paprika and season well. Pour the egg mixture evenly into the dish, then set aside to rest for about 15 minutes.

**4** Bake the casserole in the oven for 30–40 minutes until puffed up and golden brown and a skewer, when inserted, comes out clean.

# HUEVOS RANCHEROS ON TORTILLA

This all-in-one Mexican breakfast is full of fresh and vibrant flavors, and is good to eat at any time of the day.

★ **SERVES** 4

★ **PREP TIME** 20 mins

★ **COOK TIME** 15–30 mins

### Ingredients

1 x 15oz can black beans

1 tsp smoked paprika or ancho chile powder

pinch of chile flakes

salt and freshly ground black pepper

olive oil, for drizzling

4 large flour tortillas

3 cups grated Cheddar cheese

4 eggs

1 avocado, halved, pitted, and thickly sliced (see technique, p11)

### For the pico de gallo

3 large tomatoes, seeded and diced

1 jalapeño or other mild green chile, finely chopped

1 small red onion, chopped

2 garlic cloves, crushed

2 tbsp chopped cilantro leaves

juice of 2 large limes

**1** For the pico de gallo, put the tomatoes, jalapeño, onion, garlic, cilantro, and lime juice in a bowl. Season, mix well, and set aside.

**2** In a medium saucepan, gently heat the black beans in their own liquid. Stir in the smoked paprika and chile flakes, and season well.

**3** Meanwhile, heat the oil in a large, nonstick, heavy-based pan over medium heat. When the oil is hot, place a tortilla in the center of the pan. Using one-quarter of the grated cheese, make a ring inside the tortilla and crack an egg into the center, making sure that it is contained within the cheese ring.

**4** Cover and cook for 3–4 minutes until the egg starts to set and the cheese melts, then use a spatula to flip the tortilla along with the egg. Cook for 1–2 minutes for a runny yolk, and 3–4 minutes for a firm yolk. Use a spatula to lift the tortilla and the egg, flipping them egg-side up onto a plate. Clean any cheese from the pan and repeat to make the remaining tortillas.

**5** Remove the black beans from the heat and drain. Serve the tortilla and egg topped with the black beans, pico de gallo, and sliced avocado.

**COOK'S TIP** Use a wide spatula to flip the tortilla so that the egg is cradled in the middle. This will help to keep everything together. Flip quickly and confidently.

# EGGS BENEDICT WITH SMOKED SALMON

The combination of salty protein and rich, creamy sauce is irresistible in this classic breakfast dish.

★ **MAKES** 4
★ **PREP TIME** 15 mins
★ **COOK TIME** 10 mins

### Ingredients
4 eggs
2–4 English muffins
5½oz (150g) smoked salmon

### For the sauce
7 tbsp unsalted butter
1 large egg yolk
½ tbsp lemon juice
salt and freshly ground black pepper

**1** To make the hollandaise sauce, melt the butter over gentle heat, taking care it does not split. Put the egg yolk, lemon juice, and seasoning into a blender and process briefly. With the motor running, pour in the melted butter drop by drop, accelerating to a thin stream, until it has emulsified to a thick sauce.

**2** Boil a large saucepan of salted water, then reduce the heat to a low simmer. Crack an egg into a cup and gently slip the egg out of the cup and into the bubbling water. Repeat for all the eggs. Poach for 3 minutes, until the white is set but the yolk is still runny. Remove with a slotted spoon.

**3** At the same time, toast the muffins. If you like thick muffins use 4, cutting a thin slice off each one to add the egg, otherwise split 2 muffins horizontally to make 4 halves. When they are toasted, divide the salmon between them and top each with a poached egg and a little hollandaise sauce.

### WHAT'S THE STORY?
The origins of the familiar bacon version of this dish are far from clear. Two different cookbooks, both published in the 1890s, feature recipes for poached eggs and ham on a toasted muffin, smothered in hollandaise sauce. Other sources claim either the famous New York eatery Delmonico's or the Waldorf Hotel as the birth place of the dish.

## NOW TRY...

### SOURDOUGH BREAD

For a more rustic feel, serve 2 eggs, side by side, on a piece of grilled **sourdough bread**, topped with slices of **crispy bacon** and hollandaise sauce.

### EGGS FLORENTINE

For Eggs Florentine, wilt down 9oz (250g) of **baby spinach** in 1 tbsp of **olive oil**, then drain well. Mix with a spoonful of the hollandaise sauce before using it in place of the salmon.

### POTATO RÖSTIS

For a gluten-free alternative, serve the eggs and hollandaise sauce on **potato röstis**. Follow the recipe for the hashbrown nests on p66 but use the mixture to form 8 pancakes. Fry in 2 tbsp peanut or sunflower oil over medium heat for 5 minutes on each side, until crispy and cooked through.

# BAKED EGG HASHBROWN NESTS

Perfect for brunch, these hashbrown nests can be part-baked, then filled and finished at the last minute.

- ★ **MAKES** 8
- ★ **PREP TIME** 20 mins
- ★ **COOK TIME** 25–35 mins

**Ingredients**

6oz (175g) potatoes, grated weight

2½oz (75g) sweet potato, grated weight

1 small red onion, finely chopped

1¾oz (50g) pancetta, finely chopped

½ cup Cheddar cheese, coarsely grated

2 tbsp olive oil, plus extra for greasing

salt and freshly ground black pepper

8 eggs

**1** Preheat the oven to 400°F (200°C). Place the grated potatoes in a large bowl of cold water and soak them for 5 minutes to get rid of the excess starch. Drain, then put in a clean dish towel and wring to remove as much moisture as possible.

**2** Place the potatoes, onion, pancetta, and cheese in a large bowl and toss them all together. Add the oil, season well, and toss again.

**3** Lightly oil a 12-hole muffin pan. Divide the mixture evenly between 8 of the holes. Use the back of a tablespoon to push the mixture down into the pan, then up the sides. Make sure that there is enough mixture at the bottom to form a base for the eggs. The sides need to be as high as possible, as the nests will shrink slightly as they cook.

**4** Bake in the center of the oven for 15–20 minutes, until the edges are browned and a little crispy. Remove from the oven and reduce the oven temperature to 350°F (180°C).

**5** Carefully crack an egg into each of the nests, sprinkle a little pepper on top, and return to the oven for 10–15 minutes (depending on whether you like your eggs soft or hard). Remove from the oven and leave to cool in their pans for 2 minutes (the eggs will continue to cook a little more). Run a knife around the edge of each nest to loosen and remove from the pan. Serve immediately.

**COOK'S TIP** These delicious nests can also be filled with fried mushrooms, wilted spinach, or chopped crispy bacon before being topped with the eggs.

**Pancetta**, an Italian cured bacon, can be replaced with thick-cut smoked bacon.

# EGG WHITE, SPINACH, AND SALMON OMELET

Packed with protein and low in fat, these quick and easy egg white omelets are a healthy breakfast choice.

★ **SERVES** 1
★ **PREP TIME** 10 mins
★ **COOK TIME** 4–7 mins

**Ingredients**
3 egg whites
1 tbsp unsalted butter
1¾oz (50g) baby spinach,
   roughly chopped
small grating of nutmeg, or
   a pinch of dried nutmeg
freshly ground black pepper
1oz (30g) smoked salmon,
   roughly torn

**1** Put the egg whites in a large bowl and whisk with a balloon whisk or an electric hand whisk until light and frothy (see the technique below). In a large, heavy-based frying pan or omelet pan, melt the butter over medium heat. Add the spinach, season with a little grated nutmeg and pepper, and cook for 2–3 minutes, stirring frequently, until it has wilted and any moisture has evaporated.

**2** Distribute the spinach evenly around the pan and pour in the whisked egg whites. Using a heatproof spatula, move them around slightly to incorporate the spinach into the egg whites. Allow the omelet to cook over low heat for 1–2 minutes, until the edges are set and the underside is brown. Don't worry if the top still looks frothy.

**3** Arrange the smoked salmon over half of the omelet. Using a spatula, gently fold the omelet in half, so that the salmon is covered. Cook the omelet for another minute on each side, pressing down gently with the spatula, until the center is light and fluffy, but just set.

## WHISKING EGG WHITES

**1 Place the egg whites** in a large, clean, dry mixing bowl and start whisking them slowly, using a small range of motion.

**2 Continue whisking**, using larger strokes, until the whites have lost their translucency and start to foam.

**3 Incorporate as much air** as possible, increasing your speed and range of motion until the whites turn light and frothy.

# BREAKFAST BURRITOS

Stuffed with spicy and filling ingredients, these wraps are perfect for breakfast on the go.

★ **SERVES** 4
★ **PREP TIME** 20 mins
★ **COOK TIME** 50 mins

### Ingredients

2 red skinned potatoes
1 tsp olive oil
1 onion, cut into large chunks
1 red bell pepper, cut into large chunks
1 green bell pepper, cut into large chunks
1 jalapeño or other mild green chile, finely chopped
salt and freshly ground black pepper
1lb (450g) chorizo, casings removed and thickly sliced
8 eggs
1 tsp chipotle paste
2 cups grated Cheddar cheese
4 large tortillas
½ cup sour cream

### For the guacamole

1 avocado, halved, pitted, and sliced (see technique, p11)
juice of 2 limes
12 cherry tomatoes, halved
handful of chopped cilantro

**1** Cook the potatoes in a saucepan of boiling water for 10 minutes. Drain and leave to cool. Leaving the skin on, cut each potato into chunks and set aside.

**2** Heat the oil in a large, heavy-based frying pan. Add the onion, peppers, and jalapeño and toss over medium heat for about 10 minutes until starting to soften. Add the potatoes and season well. Cook, stirring occasionally, for 15–20 minutes until tender or they can be easily pierced with a fork.

**3** Meanwhile, in a separate large frying pan, cook the chorizo over medium heat for 4–5 minutes, or until browned. Remove from the pan with a slotted spoon and combine with the potatoes at the end of their cooking time.

**4** Put the eggs in a bowl, along with ¼ cup water and the chipotle paste. Season well. Using a balloon whisk or an electric hand whisk, beat the mixture until well blended. Transfer the egg mixture to the frying pan used for the chorizo. Cook the mixture, scrambling it and moving it around the pan occasionally, for 3–4 minutes or until firm. Add the cheese and stir as it melts, so that it is well incorporated.

**5** For the guacamole, mash the avocado and stir in the lime juice, tomatoes, and cilantro.

**6** Lay each tortilla on a plate and spread a spoonful of sour cream along the center line of each tortilla. Top with the potato hash, scrambled eggs, and guacamole. To make the burritos, fold the shorter ends in over the filling. Press down and fold the longer ends up over the filling, flipping the burrito over so that the shape is preserved. Serve hot.

## NOW TRY...

### VEGGIE TWIST

Substitute the chorizo with a 15oz can drained **black beans** and 1 sliced **Portobello mushroom**. Toss the mushroom and beans in 1 tbsp oil, season well, and cook in a frying pan, as directed in step 3.

### JALAPEÑO HUMMUS

Blend a 15oz can drained **chickpeas**, 1 chopped **onion**, 2 **garlic cloves**, 4 tbsp **tahini**, 1 seeded and chopped **jalapeño**, bunch of **cilantro**, pinch of **salt**, and the juice of 2 **limes**. Spread liberally over the tortillas.

### FRIED EGGS

Fry the eggs instead of scrambling. For each serving, fry 2 **eggs**, sunny side up, for 5-7 minutes, then season. Alternatively, for a classic diner breakfast, try the potato hash without the tortilla, served with a fried egg and **bacon**.

# GRILLED BANANA PBJ

A classic PBJ (peanut butter and jelly sandwich) is a childhood favorite. Add bananas and grill for an adult treat, too.

★ **MAKES** 4
★ **PREP TIME** 10 mins
★ **COOK TIME** 20 mins

### Ingredients
1 cup blackberry jam
8 slices of crusty bread
1 cup peanut butter
2 bananas, cut into
   ¼in (5mm) slices
4 tbsp butter

**1** Pour the blackberry jam into a saucepan and place it over low heat until warm. Then remove from the heat and set aside.

**2** Generously spread the slices of bread with peanut butter. Top 4 bread slices with 4 banana slices each, then cover with the remaining bread slices to make 4 sandwiches.

**3** Melt 1 tbsp of butter in a frying pan. Pan-fry the sandwiches for 2–3 minutes on each side over medium heat until crisp. Add the remaining butter to the pan, as needed, while frying the remaining sandwiches. Transfer the sandwiches to a serving plate and top with the warm jam. Serve hot.

**Bananas** sweeten while cooking, and you should choose slightly underripe ones to cook with.

# BLT WITH FRIED GREEN TOMATOES

For a gourmet BLT (bacon, lettuce, and tomato) sandwich, add crunchy fried tomatoes and this zesty lemon and basil mayo.

★ **MAKES** 1
★ **PREP TIME** 5 mins
★ **COOK TIME** 10 mins, plus 15 mins for the fried green tomatoes

### Ingredients

3 slices of applewood or other good-quality bacon
2 thickly cut slices of good-quality white bread
2 tbsp unsalted butter, softened
2 large lettuce leaves, de-ribbed and roughly chopped
4 slices of Fried green tomatoes (see p164)

### For the lemon and basil mayo

2 tbsp good-quality mayonnaise
2 tsp lemon juice
1 tbsp finely chopped basil leaves
salt and freshly ground black pepper

**1** Preheat the broiler on its highest setting. To make the lemon and basil mayo, mix together the mayonnaise, lemon juice, and basil. Season well and set aside.

**2** Preheat a grill pan or a large, cast-iron frying pan. While it is heating, broil the bacon under the broiler for 2–3 minutes on each side until crispy. Drain on paper towels and keep warm.

**3** Spread a little butter on both sides of the bread slices and grill them in the pan for 2 minutes on each side, until nicely toasted.

**4** Remove the bread slices from the heat. Spread one side of the toast with a little of the mayonnaise, then top it with the lettuce, fried green tomatoes, and the bacon. Finish with a final layer of mayonnaise and top with the second piece of bread. Cut in half to serve.

**Basil**, a sweet, fragrant herb, can be used to flavor oils and mayos.

# A taste of the
# SOUTHEAST

Encompassing coastal and mountain cooking—and with strong influences from Africa, the Caribbean, and Cuba—this region has one of the most complex and varied cuisines in the country.

The warm, damp climate of the Southeast allows for two distinct growing seasons—one in spring and a second in the fall. This double harvest is further boosted by extremely fertile soils that encourage the growth of everything from sweet potatoes and sugar cane to limes and persimmons.

The Southeast, historically a center for the slave trade, has adopted many of the culinary traditions brought to the region from Africa and the Caribbean in the 18th century. In the great culinary city of New Orleans, for example, sophisticated Creole cooking (a mixture of Spanish, French, and African cuisines) jostles for attention alongside simpler Cajun fare.

More recently, in the 1950s, immigrants from Cuba brought their own distinct foods and flavors to Florida.

**Brunswick stew—a dish with its roots firmly in the Southeast—is traditionally made with cheap, readily available meats such as squirrel and rabbit. Modern variations (see p131) are more likely to include chicken instead.**

Fried chicken, a staple of the southern food scene, tastes fantastic when home made.

## FOODS AND FLAVORS

★ **Barbecued meat** is synomynous with the Southeast, and each state has its own classic dish; the Carolinas, for example, specialize in **pulled pork** (see p130).

★ **Gumbo**, a stew-like dish made with seafood or meat (see p112), has come to symbolize the rich culinary heritage of New Orleans.

★ **Seafood**, such as the **shrimp** found in Pamlico Sound in the north, and the Florida stone crabs caught further south, is integral to the food traditions of the region.

★ **Corn**, an important crop for the Southeast, can be eaten raw when young in salads, cooked in fritters (see p25), and, when ground into cornmeal, made into cornbread (see p228) or grits (see p110).

★ **Biscuits**, a true Southern dish, can accompany any meal but are traditionally served for breakfast (see below and p58).

Creamy grits, made with either white or yellow cornmeal, are perfect with East Coast shrimp.

Light and delicate, beignets derive their name from the French version of doughnuts.

Key limes, although not native to Florida, are a speciality crop now grown throughout the region.

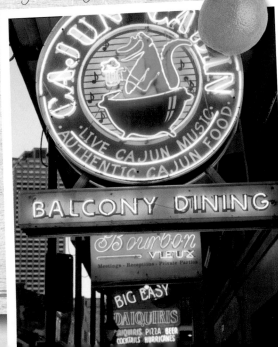

The vast Mississippi River runs all the way from northern Wisconsin to the Gulf of Mexico.

New Orleans, a melting pot of Creole and Cajun cultures, has a diverse and vibrant food scene.

# FRIED SHRIMP PO' BOYS

Shrimp or oysters are the star ingredients in this tasty and filling recipe from New Orleans.

★ **SERVES** 4
★ **PREP TIME** 10 mins
★ **COOK TIME** 18–24 mins

### Ingredients
2 loaves of French bread
8 leaves of round lettuce
1 ripe red tomato, sliced

### For the shrimp
2 cups peanut or sunflower
   oil, for frying
1 egg
1 cup all-purpose flour
1 tsp paprika
½ tsp cayenne pepper
½ tsp salt
1 cup panko breadcrumbs
   or day-old breadcrumbs
48 large shrimp, peeled
   and deveined

### For the remoulade
1 cup mayonnaise
¼ cup mustard
juice of ½ lemon
2 tbsp pickling brine or
   apple cider vinegar
1 tsp paprika
1 tbsp creamed
   horseradish

**1** In a large, heavy-based saucepan or deep-fat fryer, heat the oil to 375°F (190°C), as shown in the technique on p144.

**2** Break the egg into a bowl, add 1 tbsp water, and whisk with a fork. In a separate large bowl, mix together the flour, paprika, cayenne pepper, salt, and breadcrumbs. Dip the shrimp in the egg wash and toss them in the breadcrumb mixture, coating each one evenly.

**3** Fry in the hot oil in batches of 8 for 3–4 minutes each, or until golden brown. Remove the fried shrimp from the pan with a slotted spoon and let them cool on a wire rack.

**4** For the remoulade, combine the mayonnaise, mustard, lemon juice, vinegar, paprika, and horseradish in a bowl.

**5** Slice each loaf in half lengthwise, without cutting through the bottom, and spread the remoulade on either side. Layer each bottom half with the lettuce, sliced tomatoes, and fried shrimp. For a truly New Orleans experience, serve with potato chips tossed in Cajun seasoning.

### WHAT'S THE STORY?
The po' boy (short for "poor boy") was created by New Orleans restaurant owners and former streetcar drivers Clovis and Benjamin Martin. When streetcar drivers went on strike in 1929, the brothers served the sandwich free to unemployed workers and the cry "here comes another poor boy!" would go up in the kitchen each time.

## NOW TRY...

## BLACKENED FISH

Try making this recipe with blackened white fish, such as the **mahi-mahi** from p106, instead of shrimp.

## VEGGIE OPTION

Make vegetarian po' boys by chopping and sautéeing 1 **eggplant**, 1 **red bell pepper**, 1 **onion**, and a handful of fresh **porcini**, **button**, or **cremini mushrooms**, and season with the paprika, cayenne pepper, and salt.

## FISH & CORNMEAL

Use a white firm-fleshed fish, such as **catfish**, instead of shrimp, and substitute the breadcrumbs with 1 cup **fine polenta or cornmeal** for a cornmeal crust.

# SUMMER VEGETABLE PHILLY CHEESE STEAK

Give a lighter twist to the classic steak sandwich from Philadelphia by adding pan-fried summer vegetables.

★ **SERVES** 4

★ **PREP TIME** 10 mins, plus chilling

★ **COOK TIME** 30 mins

### Ingredients

2 tbsp butter

1 onion, chopped into large pieces

1 green bell pepper, chopped into large pieces

1 small eggplant, roughly chopped into large pieces

12 cremini or button mushrooms

½ tsp red pepper flakes

2 garlic cloves, crushed

salt and freshly ground black pepper

1lb 2oz (500g) sirloin steak, chilled for 45 minutes to make slicing easier

4 sub rolls

8 slices of provolone or Jarlsberg cheese

mustard, to serve

**1** In a heavy-based frying pan, melt 1 tbsp of the butter over medium-low heat. Add the onion, pepper, eggplant, mushrooms, red pepper flakes, and garlic. Season well. Cook the vegetables, stirring occasionally, for 15–20 minutes, or until tender.

**2** Meanwhile, cut the steak into paper-thin slices. In a separate heavy-based frying pan, heat the remaining butter and cook the steak over medium-high heat. Add a pinch of salt and cook the meat, stirring occasionally, for 3–5 minutes, or until browned.

**3** Slice each sub roll in half lengthwise, without cutting through the bottom, and line each roll with 2 slices of cheese. Add the vegetables and top with the steak. Serve hot with mustard.

**Eggplants** are at their best when the skin is very smooth and they feel heavy for their size.

# SHRIMP AND SWEET POTATO QUESADILLAS

These Mexican inspired hot tortilla sandwiches are quick and easy to prepare—and incredibly delicious.

★ **MAKES** 4
★ **PREP TIME** 20 mins
★ **COOK TIME** 45 mins

**Ingredients**

2 large sweet potatoes
3 tbsp olive oil
1 garlic clove, crushed
1lb 5oz (600g) large shrimp, cooked and peeled
8 x 12in (30cm) large tortillas
2 cups Monterey Jack or cheddar cheese, grated
salt and freshly ground black pepper
1 tsp smoked paprika or ancho chili powder
1 avocado, halved, pitted, and peeled (see technique, p11)
½ cup sour cream
juice of 1 lime
bunch of cilantro, chopped

**1** Cook the potatoes in a pan of boiling water, skin-on, for 20 minutes. Drain the potatoes and set them aside to cool. When cool enough to handle, peel, cut into cubes, and set aside.

**2** Heat 1 tbsp of the oil in a deep, straight-sided frying pan. Add the garlic, along with the potatoes, and cook over medium heat for 5–10 minutes, or until the potatoes have browned. Add the shrimp and reduce the heat. Stir to incorporate.

**3** Lay out 4 tortillas and spread equal portions of the shrimp and potato mixture on them and top with the grated cheese. Sprinkle each tortilla with salt, pepper, and smoked paprika. Top with the remaining tortillas to create 4 "sandwiches" or quesadillas.

**4** Heat another tbsp of oil in a large, nonstick, heavy-based pan. Cook the quesadilla for 2–3 minutes on each side, or until browned and the cheese has melted. Add the remaining oil to the pan, as needed, while cooking the remaining quesadillas.

**5** In a bowl, mash the avocado with the back of a fork to the desired consistency. Mix together the sour cream, avocado, lime juice, and cilantro. Top the quesadillas with the avocado cream, slice into quarters, and serve hot.

**Tortillas**, either wheat- or corn-based, are a great alternative to more traditional breads.

# FLANK STEAK AND CHEDDAR BURRITOS

Bursting with meat, vegetables, rice, beans, and cheese, these burritos are the ultimate meal in one simple package.

★ **MAKES** 4
★ **PREP TIME** 20 mins
★ **COOK TIME** 20 mins

### Ingredients

5½oz (150g) green bell pepper, seeded and sliced
9oz (250g) onion, sliced
1 tbsp olive oil
1lb (450g) flank steak
salt and freshly ground black pepper
1 tbsp chipotle paste
4 x 12in (30cm) large tortillas
1 cup white rice, cooked
1 cup black beans, cooked
1 cup sharp cheddar cheese, crumbled
2 avocados, halved, pitted, and peeled (see technique, p11)

### For the salsa verde

7oz (200g) green tomatoes, roughly chopped
1 onion, about 5½oz (150g), diced
1¼oz (40g) cilantro
1oz (30g) jalapeño or other mild green chile, seeded and chopped
2 garlic cloves, roughly chopped
juice of 2 limes

**1** First, make the salsa verde. In a food processor, pulse the tomatoes, onion, cilantro, jalapeño, garlic, lime juice, and seasoning to make a smooth purée. Set aside.

**2** In a large frying pan, sauté the pepper and onion in ½ tbsp of oil over high heat. Cook for 5–7 minutes, stirring frequently, or until tender and crisp. Remove from the pan and set aside.

**3** Sprinkle both sides of the steak with salt and pepper and spread the chipotle paste evenly all over. Cook over medium-high heat in the remaining oil for 4–10 minutes on each side, depending on how you like your meat. For rare, allow 4–6 minutes on each side; for medium, 6–8 minutes; and for well done, 8–10 minutes. Remove from the pan and let it rest for 5 minutes before cutting into slices.

**4** Lay out the tortillas. Layer each one with the rice, beans, sautéed vegetables, steak, cheddar cheese, and salsa verde, keeping the ingredients piled in the middle of the tortilla. To make the burritos, fold the shorter ends in over the filling, then press down and roll the longer ends over each other, flipping the burrito over so that the shape is preserved. Return the burritos, seam-side down, to the pan and cook for 2–3 minutes on each side.

**5** In a grill pan, grill the avocados over medium-high heat for 3–4 minutes. Serve the burritos hot with the salsa verde and avocado on the side.

# DELI-STYLE REUBEN

This sandwich is piled high with classic deli fillings, contrasting sweet, sour, and salty flavors.

★ **SERVES** 4
★ **PREP TIME** 10 mins
★ **COOK TIME** 10 mins

### Ingredients

8 slices of rye bread
16 slices of Swiss or
  Emmental cheese
1lb (450g) corned beef
  or pastrami
8 tbsp sauerkraut (see
  p245), or from a jar
4 pats of butter

### For the Russian dressing

¼ cup mayonnaise
2 tbsp creamed
  horseradish
1 tbsp ketchup
1 tsp Worcestershire sauce
salt and freshly ground
  black pepper

**1** In a bowl, mix together the mayonnaise, horseradish, ketchup, and Worcestershire sauce. Season well.

**2** Spread the dressing over each slice of bread. Layer 4 slices of bread with 2 slices of cheese, 3–5 slices of beef, sauerkraut, and 2 more slices of cheese. Top with the remaining slices of bread.

**3** Melt a pat of butter in a frying pan over medium heat. Fry each sandwich for 1–2 minutes on each side, or until golden brown. Serve your Reuben hot with Refrigerator pickles (see p248) and kettle-cooked potato chips.

### WHAT'S THE STORY?

Tales abound about who invented this sandwich, with Arnold Reuben of Reuben's Delicatessen in New York City and Reuben Kulakofsky, a grocer from Omaha, Nebraska, both strong contenders. The first Reuben was probably made in the early 20th century and, by 1956, it had won "best sandwich" in a contest sponsored by the National Restaurant Association.

## NOW TRY...

### PASTRAMI ON RYE

Make pastrami on rye by layering **pastrami**, **Swiss cheese**, and **brown mustard**. Melt **butter** in a pan and grill the sandwich to melt the cheese and warm the pastrami.

### TURKEY

Make this a "Rachael" instead of a Reuben by substituting the corned beef with an equal amount of **turkey**.

### FRIED EGG TOPPING

Complete your Reuben by placing a **fried egg**, sunny-side up, on top of the cheese slices.

# SALAMI MUFFULETTAS WITH RED PEPPERS

This classic New Orleans-style layered sandwich is given a Mediterranean twist with a layer of roasted pepper tapenade.

★ **SERVES** 4

★ **PREP TIME** 30 mins, plus marinating

### Ingredients

1 loaf Italian-style seasame seed bread

2¼ cups mozzarella cheese

1 cup provolone or Jarlsberg cheese

3oz (85g) salami, thinly sliced

1 cup mortadella, thinly sliced

3oz (85g) Parma ham, thinly sliced

### For the tapenade

3½oz (100g) pitted green olives, chopped

2 roasted red peppers (see technique, right), chopped

1 shallot, sliced

2 tbsp olive oil

2 tsp red wine vinegar

1 tbsp capers

pinch each of chopped thyme, rosemary, and oregano

salt and freshly ground black pepper

**1** For the tapenade, stir together the olives, peppers, shallot, oil, vinegar, capers, and the herbs in a medium bowl. Season well. Leave to marinate for 10 minutes.

**2** Slice the loaf in half horizontally. Scoop out one-third of the bread from the insides of the top and bottom halves. Spread the olive mixture evenly across the top and bottom.

**3** Layer the cheeses and meats onto the bottom half of the loaf. Replace the top and press down well. Wrap in plastic wrap and marinate the sandwich for at least 1 hour, or keep chilled for up to 1 day. Cut into slices to serve.

## ROASTING AND PEELING PEPPER

**1 With a pair of tongs**, hold the pepper over an open flame to char the skin. Rotate the pepper and char each side evenly.

**2 Put the pepper** into a plastic bag, seal, and allow the skin to loosen. When the pepper has cooled, peel away the charred skin.

# PRETZELDOGS WITH CHEDDAR AND ALE DIP

These pretzeldogs are equally good served with the dip for adults, or simply with ketchup for children.

★ **MAKES** 8

★ **PREP TIME** 30 mins, plus rising and proving

★ **COOK TIME** 30 mins, plus cooling

### Ingredients

1¼ cup strong white bread flour, plus extra for dusting

¾ cup all-purpose flour

½ tsp salt

1 tbsp sugar

1 tsp dried yeast

½ tbsp peanut or sunflower oil, plus extra for greasing

8 sausages or hot dogs

mustard (optional)

coarse sea salt

### For the Cheddar and ale dip

10fl oz (300ml) pale ale

1 cup grated sharp cheddar cheese

2 heaped tbsp all-purpose flour

2 tbsp heavy cream

1 heaped tbsp Dijon mustard

1 heaped tbsp honey

salt and freshly ground black pepper

1 Put the flours, salt, and sugar into a mixing bowl. In a separate bowl, sprinkle the yeast over ⅔ cup warm water. Stir once, leave for 5 minutes until dissolved, then add the oil.

2 Pour the liquid into the flour mixture, stirring it together to form a soft dough. Knead for 10 minutes on a floured work surface until pliable. Put in a lightly oiled bowl, cover loosely with plastic wrap, and leave in a warm place for 1–2 hours until nearly doubled in size.

3 Turn out the dough onto a floured work surface and knock it back. Divide it into 8 equal pieces. Take each piece of dough and roll it under your palm to form a log shape. Using your palms, continue to roll the dough outward toward each end, until it is about 18in (46cm) long. If the dough is difficult to stretch, hold it by either end and gently rotate it in a looping action as you would a jump rope.

4 Take each sausage and brush with a little mustard (if using). Starting at the top, wrap the pretzel dough around the sausage in a circular twisting motion, so that it is completely sealed in, with only the top and the bottom showing. Pinch the dough together at the top and bottom to make sure it doesn't unwrap.

5 Place on baking sheets lined with parchment paper, cover with oiled plastic wrap and a dish towel, and leave in a warm place for about 30 minutes until well puffed up. Preheat the oven to 400°F (200°C). Scatter the pretzeldogs with sea salt and bake for 15 minutes until golden brown and shiny. Remove from the oven and cool on a wire rack for 5 minutes before serving.

6 For the dip, bring the ale to a boil in a medium, heavy-based saucepan. Meanwhile, toss the cheddar cheese with the flour until well combined (this will help to thicken the sauce). When the ale begins to boil, reduce the heat to low and whisk in the cheese. Cook over low heat, whisking constantly, until the cheese melts. Add the cream, mustard, and honey to the sauce and season to taste. Cook for a further 3–5 minutes, whisking frequently, until the sauce thickens. Serve warm with the pretzeldogs.

# BACON, ONION, AND CHEESE HOT DOGS

Using caramelized onion, melted cheese, and pickled cucumber takes an everyday hot dog to another level.

★ **MAKES** 4
★ **PREP TIME** 10 mins
★ **COOK TIME** 45–50 mins

**Ingredients**

3 tbsp olive oil
2 red onions, thinly sliced
1 tbsp sugar
3 tbsp balsamic vinegar
salt and freshly ground
   black pepper
4 slices of good-quality smoked
   bacon
4 good-quality thick hot dogs, or
   other smoked sausages
4 tbsp mild sweet mustard
½ cup grated Gruyère cheese
4 large hot dog buns
4 tbsp finely chopped pickled
   cucumbers (see Refrigerator
   pickles, p249), to serve

**1** Heat the oil in a medium, heavy-based frying pan over low heat. Add the onions and cook for 15 minutes, until softened but not browned. Add the sugar, vinegar, 2 tbsp water, and season well. Continue to cook for 15 minutes, or until the onions are sweet and sticky. Set aside.

**2** Preheat the broiler on its highest setting. Run the blade of a large knife along the surface of each bacon slice to stretch out the bacon if it is thickly cut; this will help it wrap easily around the sausage. Thinly cut bacon can be used as it is. Prick each sausage a couple of times with a fork, then wrap a slice of bacon around each one, in a spiral fashion, so that the meat is covered with the bacon.

**3** Place the wrapped sausages, join-side down, on a baking sheet and broil for 10–15 minutes, turning only after the top is crispy and brown. When they are crispy all over, remove from the broiler. Spread 1 tbsp of the mustard on top of each sausage. Arrange them together on the baking sheet, so that they are touching each other and sprinkle all over with the cheese, being sure to mound it up along each sausage. Return them to the broiler and cook briefly until the cheese is melted.

**4** To serve, spread a quarter of the caramelized red onions into each hot dog bun, top with a bacon and cheese sausage, and sprinkle 1 tbsp of the pickled cucumbers along the top.

**COOK'S TIP** These would also taste good when served with some Quick stovetop sauerkraut (see p245) instead of the caramelized red onions.

### WHAT'S THE STORY?

A hot dog is simply a cooked sausage—typically either a frankfurter or wiener—in a sliced bun. There is little doubt that hot sausages were first sold on the streets of the United States by German immigrants in the mid to late 19th century, although stories differ as to the identity of their creator. Most accounts agree that hot dogs first appeared in New York City.

# PULLED CHICKEN TACOS

Cooking a whole chicken like this gives a moist, flavorsome result. Use leftovers in salads or wraps.

★ **SERVES** 4
★ **PREP TIME** 30–40 mins
★ **COOK TIME** 1½ hrs

### Ingredients

1 small whole chicken, about 3lb (1.35kg)
2 tbsp apple cider vinegar
1 tbsp chile flakes
salt and freshly ground black pepper
1 small red onion, quartered
4 garlic cloves
8 corn tortillas

### For the chicken sauce

¼ cup apple cider vinegar
pinch of chile flakes
1 tsp smoked paprika powder

### For the pico de gallo

3 large tomatoes, seeded and diced
1 jalapeño or other mild green chile, finely chopped
1 small red onion, chopped
2 garlic cloves, crushed
½ bunch of cilantro chopped
juice of 2 large limes

### For the pickled onions

1 red onion, thinly sliced
1 cup apple cider vinegar

### For the avocado cream

1 cup Greek yogurt
½ avocado, very ripe, peeled
juice of 1 lime
handful of cilantro, chopped

**1** Preheat the oven to 325°F (160°C). Put the chicken (breast-side down), vinegar, chile flakes, 1 tbsp salt, onion, and garlic in a flameproof casserole or Dutch oven. Add 1¾ pints (1 liter) of water and cook in the oven for 1½ hours.

**2** For the pico de gallo, mix together the tomatoes, jalapeño, onion, garlic, cilantro, and lime juice in a bowl. Season with salt to taste and set aside to let the flavors blend.

**3** For the pickled onions, put the onion, vinegar, and 1 tbsp salt in a nonreactive saucepan (not aluminum or cast iron) over medium heat. Simmer until the onion is translucent and light pink in color. Remove from the heat to cool.

**4** For the avocado cream, put the yogurt, avocado, lime juice, and cilantro in a small bowl. Mash together with a fork until creamy. Season with a pinch of salt.

**5** Remove the chicken from its cooking liquid, pull the meat from the bones, and discard the skin (reserve the bones for making stock). Using your hands, or two forks, shred the chicken. Toss with the vinegar, chile flakes, and paprika. Season to taste.

**6** Drain the pico de gallo through a fine mesh strainer. Layer the avocado cream, chicken, pico de gallo, and pickled onions on top of the tortillas and serve.

## NOW TRY...

### SHRIMP & TEQUILA

Toss 14oz (400g) **shrimp** with
2 tbsp **tequila**, the juice of
1 **lime**, and a pinch of **salt** and grill
for 5–7 minutes, or until pink.

### STEAK TACOS

Try these tacos with the **dry-rub
steak** from p128, instead of
the chicken.

### CABBAGE SLAW

Make a quick cabbage slaw by combining
½ shredded small **red cabbage**, 1 shaved
**carrot**, 1 sliced **red onion**, 3 tbsp **apple
cider vinegar**, and a pinch of **sea salt**.
Add as an extra layer to your tacos.

# CURRIED LAMB SLOPPY JOES WITH NAAN BREAD

Gently spiced lamb is topped with herby yogurt and stuffed into warm bread for a new take on an old favorite.

★ **SERVES** 4
★ **PREP TIME** 20 mins
★ **COOK TIME** 50 mins

**Ingredients**
2 tbsp olive oil
1 small onion, finely chopped
1 carrot, finely diced
½ celery stalk, finely diced
2 garlic cloves, finely chopped
2in (5cm) piece of ginger,
    finely chopped
1 jalapeño or other mild
    green chile, seeded and
    finely chopped
1lb 2oz (500g) ground lamb
½ tsp ground cilantro
½ tsp cayenne pepper
½ tsp ground cinnamon
1 tsp ground cumin
1 tsp plain flour
2 cups hot chicken stock
salt and freshly ground
    black pepper
3 tbsp roughly chopped
    mint leaves
3 tbsp roughly chopped cilantro
6 heaped tbsp Greek yogurt
1 scallion, trimmed
    and finely chopped
4 warm naan breads, halved

**1** Heat the oil in a large, heavy-based frying pan over medium heat. Add the onion, carrot, and celery and cook for 10 minutes, until softened but not browned. Add the garlic, ginger, and jalapeño and cook for a further 2 minutes.

**2** Increase the heat and add the lamb, breaking it down with a spoon as it goes into the pan. Cook for 5 minutes, constantly stirring to break up the meat, until well browned and separated. Sprinkle over the dried spices and the flour, and cook for a further minute or two.

**3** Add the stock and stir well to combine. Bring to a boil, then reduce the heat to a low simmer and cook, uncovered, for 30–35 minutes until the liquid has evaporated and the lamb is tender. Season to taste and remove from the heat. Stir in 2 tbsp each of the chopped mint and cilantro.

**4** In a small bowl, mix together the Greek yogurt, the remaining herbs, and the scallion and season to taste. To serve, spoon a portion of the meat on one half of the naan bread. Add a spoonful of the yogurt mixture and top with the other half of the naan bread.

**COOK'S TIP** This lamb curry is also delicious served over rice with a chopped herby cucumber and tomato salad on the side, and a squeeze of lime.

### WHAT'S THE STORY?

A traditional Sloppy Joe (so-called because it's messy to eat) comprises ground beef, onions, tomatoes, and seasoning, cooked down and stuffed into a bun. References to the dish date back to the depression era of the 1930s, when meat was a precious commodity, and the sandwich may have been created as a way to make a little meat go a long way.

# GRILLED CHEESE SANDWICH

Buttering the outside gives this sandwich a crunch that contrasts well with the melting cheese.

★ **MAKES** 1
★ **PREP TIME** 5 mins
★ **COOK TIME** 5 mins

### Ingredients

2 thick slices of good-quality white bread
2 tbsp unsalted butter, softened
¼ cup grated good-quality sharp cheese, such as Cheddar

**1** Preheat a grill pan or large, cast-iron frying pan. Spread a little butter on one side of each slice of bread and grill for 2 minutes, buttered-side down, until the bread is lightly toasted.

**2** Remove the bread from the heat. Butter the other sides lightly, being sure to spread the butter all the way to the edges.

**3** Turn the bread over to the lightly grilled side and spread the grated cheese evenly over one slice, then top it with the other slice, so that the pre-grilled sides are inside and the buttered ones outside.

**4** Return the sandwich to the pan and grill for 2–3 minutes on each side, pressing down lightly with a spatula to ensure that the cheese melts. The sandwich is ready when it is golden brown and crispy, and the cheese has melted. Serve alongside Creamy tomato soup with corn and peppers (see p33).

**COOK'S TIP** When grilling, move the sandwich as little as possible. If you turn the sandwich more than once, it will be difficult to keep the grill marks aligned.

**Sharp Cheddar**, with its strong, earthy flavor, brings a simple sandwich to life.

## NOW TRY...

# APPLE & MAPLE SYRUP

Before grilling the bread, peel, core, slice, and grill 1 **sharp apple**, such as Granny Smith, until golden brown. Brush it with **maple syrup** and add it to the sandwich, along with 3 slices of **crispy bacon** for the ultimate in comfort food.

# GRUYÈRE, HAM, & EGG

For a quick lunch, grill sliced **Gruyère** and 2oz (60g) **smoked ham** in **sourdough bread**, and top with a crispy **fried egg** for an updated Croque Madame.

# BRIE & CRANBERRY

Try making a grilled cheese sandwich using **walnut bread**, thickly sliced **brie** (trimmed), and 1 tbsp **cranberry sauce** from p165.

# MAINS AND SIDES

# GARLIC BUTTERED ROASTED TURKEY

## Taking the time to brine a turkey for a whole day before cooking produces a moist, flavorful result.

★ **SERVES** 6

★ **PREP TIME** 10 mins, plus brining

★ **COOK TIME** 2½ hrs, plus resting

### Ingredients
6–10lb (2.7–5kg) whole turkey
2 garlic bulbs
1 cup butter, softened
salt and freshly ground
   black pepper

### For the brine
⅔ cup sea salt
2 bay leaves
1 tbsp allspice
pinch of cayenne pepper
5 garlic cloves, crushed
4 lemons, sliced

**1** Prepare the brine a day in advance by filling a large stock pot or flameproof casserole halfway with water and stirring in the sea salt, bay leaves, allspice, cayenne pepper, garlic, and lemons.

**2** Add the turkey to the brine, making sure that it is completely submerged. Cover the pot with a lid, set aside in a cool dark place, and let it sit overnight.

**3** The next day, preheat the oven to 475°F (240°C). Remove the bird from the brine and pat dry. Using a paring knife, cut small slits throughout the turkey, particularly in the breast and legs. Peel one bulb of garlic and stuff a garlic clove into each slit.

**4** Using your hands, generously massage the butter into the skin of the turkey. If possible, lift the skin and spread it underneath. Slice the remaining bulb of garlic in half and place it in the cavity. Season well and place the turkey, breast-side up, in a large roasting pan.

**5** Roast the turkey in the oven for 20 minutes, then lower the oven temperature to 375°F (190°C). Roast for a further 2 hours, or until a thermometer inserted into the breast reads 330°F (165°C). Check the temperature frequently to prevent the meat from burning. Remove the turkey from the oven and let it rest for at least 30 minutes before carving and serving with other Thanksgiving dishes, such as Sweet potato casserole (see p162) or Green bean casserole (see p149).

### WHAT'S THE STORY?
Turkey has become synonymous with Thanksgiving, and the foods served during the traditional celebratory dinner are meant to imitate the meals of the early settlers. However, it is likely that those 17th-century settlers actually ate more duck, goose, and venison than turkey. Thanksgiving was declared a national holiday by President Lincoln in 1863.

# BOURBON AND BROWN SUGAR BBQ CHICKEN

A classic barbecue sauce is given a lift with the addition of bourbon, or whisky, for a deep, smoky flavor when grilled.

★ **SERVES** 4
★ **PREP TIME** 5 mins
★ **COOK TIME** 30 mins

### Ingredients

1 cup ketchup
¾ cup apple cider vinegar
¼ cup bourbon
½ cup light brown sugar
1 tsp mustard powder
1 tsp cayenne pepper
  or paprika
1 tsp garlic powder
1 tsp sea salt
8 skin-on, bone-in
  chicken thighs
Boston baked beans
  (see p146), spinach, and
  4 corn cobs, to serve

**1** In a medium bowl, whisk together the ketchup, vinegar, bourbon, sugar, spices, and sea salt. Set aside some of the sauce for glazing and generously baste the chicken all over with the rest.

**2** Cook the chicken under a medium-hot broiler for 12–15 minutes on each side, or until cooked through, basting regularly. Alternatively, preheat the oven to 350°F (180°C) and bake the chicken for 25–30 minutes, or until cooked through. Using a clean brush, baste the reserved sauce over the cooked chicken, and serve hot with Boston baked beans, spinach, and corn cobs.

# SOUTHERN FRIED CHICKEN

The trick for keeping this dish crisp, light, and juicy is to maintain the oil at the correct temperature.

★ **SERVES** 4
★ **PREP TIME** 20 mins, plus soaking and resting
★ **COOK TIME** 15 mins

**Ingredients**

2 cups buttermilk (or to make your own, see p12)
1 tbsp hot sauce
8 skin-on chicken pieces, preferably legs and small thighs
1 cup self-rising flour
2 tbsp cornstarch
1 tsp salt
1 tsp garlic powder
1 tsp cayenne pepper
1 tsp paprika
1 tsp black pepper
1¾ pints (1 liter) peanut or sunflower oil, for frying

**1** Whisk together the buttermilk and hot sauce, and season well. Put the chicken pieces into a dish in a single layer and pour the buttermilk over them. Cover the dish in plastic wrap and chill for at least 4 hours, or preferably overnight.

**2** When you are ready to cook the chicken, put all the dry ingredients together in a large plastic bag and shake well to combine. Take the chicken pieces out of the buttermilk mixture and shake off any excess. Put the chicken pieces into the bag, one at a time, and shake until they are well covered with the coating. Lay them on a wire rack as you work, and allow them to rest for 30 minutes at room temperature (this will help the coating to stick during frying).

**3** In a large, heavy-based saucepan or deep-fat fryer, heat the oil to 375°F (190°C) and carefully lower the chicken pieces into the oil, without overcrowding the pan. Cook for 5–7 minutes on each side (depending on the size of the pieces), turning them over occasionally so that they brown evenly. The temperature of the oil will dip when the chicken is added, and should be maintained at 300–325°F (150–160°C). The chicken is ready if the juices run clear when a skewer is inserted into the thickest part of the meat.

**4** Remove the chicken pieces from the pan with a slotted spoon and drain well on a piece of paper towel. If you are cooking in more than one batch, keep the fried chicken warm in the oven at 300°F (150°C) while you cook the remaining pieces.

## NOW TRY...

# CORNFLAKE COATING

Replace the flour with 2 cups **cornflakes**. Put them in the bag with the spices, crush them with a rolling pin, then coat and fry the chicken as directed.

# CHICKEN NUGGETS

For a kids' treat, dice 1lb 2oz (500g) of **chicken breast**, and coat and fry them, as directed, for 5–7 minutes. Serve with a **spicy dipping sauce**.

# BAKED CHICKEN

Substitute ½ cup of the flour with an equal amount of **panko breadcrumbs**. Heat 4 tbsp of oil in a roasting pan at 350°F (180°C) in the oven until sizzling hot. Add the chicken, bake for 40 minutes until golden brown, and serve with **potato fries**.

# BISCUIT-TOPPED CHICKEN POT PIE

## Biscuits make a quick and easy alternative to shortcrust pastry when topping a pie.

★ **SERVES** 6-8
★ **PREP TIME** 30 mins
★ **COOK TIME** 1 hr

### Ingredients

3 tbsp olive oil
12oz (350g) skinless, boneless chicken breast
3 garlic cloves, crushed
1 tsp chipotle paste
1 large onion, finely chopped
3 carrots, about 3½oz (100g) each, cut into ½in (1cm) slices
2 potatoes, about 3oz (85g) each, cut into cubes
1 small sweet potato, about 3½oz (100g), peeled and finely diced
9oz (250g) corn kernels, or 12oz (340g) can corn, drained
9oz (250g) peas
salt and freshly ground black pepper
3 tbsp all-purpose flour
1 cup whole milk
1 cup hot chicken stock
½ cup heavy cream

### For the biscuits

2½ cups all-purpose flour, plus extra for dusting
2 tsp baking powder
1 tsp salt
1 cup grated cheddar cheese
¼ cup vegetable shortening
1 cup whole milk
1 egg, lightly beaten, for glazing

**1** In a frying pan, heat 1 tbsp of the oil and brown the chicken breast over medium heat for 2–3 minutes on each side. Remove from the pan and set aside to cool. When cool enough to handle, cut the chicken breast into cubes.

**2** Heat the remaining oil in a flameproof casserole over medium heat and sauté the garlic. Add the chipotle paste, onion, carrots, the potatoes, corn, and peas. Season well. Cook, stirring occasionally, until the onion turns translucent.

**3** Add the flour and stir, then add the chicken, milk, stock, and cream. Stir together and simmer for 15 minutes on low heat, until the sauce has thickened.

**4** Meanwhile, preheat the oven to 350°F (180°C). For the biscuits, mix together the flour, baking powder, salt, and cheese in a large bowl. Rub the vegetable shortening into the flour mixture with your fingertips until it resembles breadcrumbs. Make a well in the center of the mixture, pour in the milk, and mix together until well combined.

**5** Gently knead the mixture on a floured work surface to form a soft dough. Roll out the dough to a thickness of ½in (1cm). Cut rounds out of the dough with a 2½in (6cm) biscuit cutter.

**6** Place the biscuits over the pie mixture in the casserole and brush each biscuit with a little beaten egg. Bake for 35–40 minutes, or until the biscuits are golden brown and the pie is bubbling. Serve hot.

# CHICKEN WITH ROSEMARY DUMPLINGS

Add as many vegetables as you like to this great family favorite, and vary the herbs in the dumplings if you prefer.

★ **SERVES** 6-8
★ **PREP TIME** 30 mins
★ **COOK TIME** 3 hrs

## Ingredients

2¾lb (1.25kg) skin-on,
   bone-in chicken thighs
1 tbsp olive oil
3 garlic cloves, crushed
10oz (300g) onion,
   roughly chopped
3-4 celery stalks, sliced
3 tbsp all-purpose flour
7oz (200g) mushrooms, halved
salt and freshly ground
   black pepper
1 cup dry white wine
1 tbsp apple cider vinegar
7oz (200g) peas

## For the dumplings

2 cups all-purpose flour
1 tsp baking powder
½ tsp salt
2 tbsp butter, cut into cubes
1 cup whole milk
1 tbsp chopped rosemary,
   plus extra to garnish

**1** If you prefer, remove the skin from the chicken thighs, and in a large soup pot, brown the chicken pieces over high heat for 1 minute on each side. Remove from the pot and set aside.

**2** Add the oil to the pot and add the garlic, onion, and celery. Cook over medium heat for 4–5 minutes, or until the onions and celery soften. Stir in the flour, mushrooms, and seasoning. Add the wine, vinegar, and 4 cups of water and bring to a boil. Return the chicken to the pot, reduce the heat, and simmer, covered, for 2½–3 hours.

**3** When the chicken is falling off the bone, remove it from the pot using a slotted spoon and transfer to a plate. Discard the skin (if kept on) and shred the chicken using a fork. Discard the bones and return the chicken to the pot. Season to taste.

**4** For the dumplings, mix the flour, baking powder, and salt. Rub the butter into the flour mixture with your fingertips until it resembles breadcrumbs. Make a well in the center, stir in the milk and rosemary, and mix to form a wet batter.

**5** Use a spoon to form 10–12 rough balls and gently drop them into the simmering stew, along with the peas. Cover and cook for 12–15 minutes, or until the dumplings are puffed up and cooked. Serve hot, in individual bowls, garnished with the remaining rosemary.

**Rosemary** is tougher than most culinary herbs, and should be chopped as finely as possible.

# HOPPIN' JOHN

Spicy jalapeño and shredded kale pep up this simple dish of rice and beans, traditionally made with collard greens.

★ **SERVES** 4-6
★ **PREP TIME** 15 mins
★ **COOK TIME** 2 hrs

### Ingredients

8 thick-cut smoked bacon slices
3 garlic cloves, crushed
1 onion, roughly chopped
1 green bell pepper,
    roughly chopped
3 celery stalks, roughly chopped
7oz (200g) kale, de-ribbed and
    roughly chopped
1 jalapeño or other mild green
    chile, finely chopped
1 tsp white pepper
1 tsp red pepper flakes
1 tsp dried oregano
salt
pat of butter
½ cup apple cider vinegar
1lb (450g) dried black-eyed
    beans
4 cups long-grain white rice
1 scallion, chopped,
    to garnish

**1** Cook the bacon over medium heat in a Dutch oven, heavy-based soup pot, or flameproof casserole. Stir in the garlic. Add the onion, green bell pepper, celery, and kale. Next, add the jalapeño, white pepper, red pepper flakes, oregano, and ½ tbsp salt, or to taste.

**2** Cook, stirring occasionally, for 7–10 minutes until the onions and peppers have softened. If the mixture begins to stick to the pan, add some butter, as needed.

**3** Add the vinegar, beans, and 1¾ pints (1 liter) of water. Reduce the heat to a simmer, cover, and cook for 1–2 hours, until the beans are softened but not mushy.

**4** About 20 minutes before the end of cooking time, bring 1¾ pints (1 liter) of water to a boil in a large, heavy-based saucepan. Add a pinch of salt and stir in the rice. Increase the heat to high and bring the water back to a boil. Cover, reduce to low heat, and simmer until the rice has absorbed the water and softened.

**5** Spoon the rice into a serving dish and top with the beans. Garnish with the chopped scallions and serve hot.

### ★★★ WHAT'S THE STORY?

Served at New Year in the South, Hoppin' John is said to bring prosperity for the coming year, with the beans resembling coins and the collard greens representing the color of money. As for the name, some say that children hopped around waiting for it to be served; others that it was once sold on the streets of Charleston, SC, by a lame character known as "Hopping" John.

# TOMATO, BASIL, AND MOZZARELLA PIZZA

This thin-crust pizza has a bright and breezy West Coast feel with the use of fresh tomatoes and herbs.

- ★ **MAKES** 2
- ★ **PREP TIME** 30 mins, plus rising
- ★ **COOK TIME** 15–20 mins

### Ingredients

2¼ tsps active dried yeast
1 tsp sugar
3 cups all-purpose flour, plus extra for dusting
1 tsp salt
3 tbsp olive oil, plus extra for greasing
2 tbsp fine polenta or cornmeal, for dusting

### For the topping

3 tbsp olive oil
6 ripe plum tomatoes, skinned and finely chopped
2 garlic cloves, crushed
salt and freshly ground black pepper
1¼ cup thinly sliced mozzarella
handful of basil leaves, roughly torn

**1** Whisk the yeast and sugar in 1 cup of warm water until the yeast has dissolved. Cover with plastic wrap or a clean dish towel and leave for 5 minutes until the surface is frothy.

**2** Sift together the flour and salt into a large bowl. Make a well in the center and mix in the yeast mixture, along with the oil. Bring the mixture together and add a little more water, if needed, to form a soft, pliable dough.

**3** By hand or in a food processor with a dough hook, knead the dough for 5–10 minutes, until smooth and elastic. Place it in a lightly oiled bowl, cover it tightly with plastic wrap and a clean dish towel, and leave it to rise for 30–45 minutes, or until doubled in size.

**4** Meanwhile, make the tomato sauce. In a large, heavy-based frying pan, heat the oil over medium heat and add the tomatoes and garlic. Season well and cook over medium heat for 5 minutes, or until the tomatoes have broken down and any liquid has evaporated to leave a thick paste. (If the tomatoes are not ripe, try adding a pinch of sugar and 1 tsp of tomato paste to enhance the flavors of the sauce.) Set aside to cool.

**5** Preheat the oven to 475°F (240°C). Scatter two 12in (30cm) square baking trays with 1 tbsp each of the polenta. Place the dough on a floured surface and knock it back. Divide it into 2 equal pieces and roll out the pizzas to a diameter of 11–12in (28–30cm).

**6** Place the rolled out pizzas on the prepared trays and stretch them to fit the tray. Divide the tomato sauce equally between the pizzas, then scatter the mozzarella evenly over the surface. Bake for 10–12 minutes until the surface is bubbling and crispy at the edges, and the base is crisp. Finish by scattering the basil over the pizzas.

## NOW TRY...

### PARMA HAM

Try topping each cooked pizza with 2-3 slices of **Parma ham**, roughly torn, and a handful of **baby arugula leaves**, drizzled with good-quality **olive oil**.

### RICOTTA SAUCE

As an alternative to the tomato sauce, use 1½ cups **ricotta cheese**, mixed with a handful of finely chopped **basil leaves** and the zest of 1 **lemon**. Season well. Spread over the base of the pizzas, top with slices of **prosciutto**, and cook as directed.

### GRILLED CHICKEN

Cover the tomato topping with 5½oz (150g) of thinly sliced, grilled **chicken breast**, 1 tbsp finely chopped **rosemary**, and 6 tbsp of **mascarpone** mixed with 4 tbsp of grated **Parmesan cheese** before baking.

# CHICKEN PARMESAN SLIDERS

Sliders are essentially mini burgers, and these chicken versions make great party food for friends and family.

★ **MAKES** 8
★ **PREP TIME** 30 mins
★ **COOK TIME** 55 mins

### Ingredients

2 chicken breasts, about
   5oz (140g) each
¼ cup olive oil, for dipping, plus
   extra for frying and brushing
8 slider buns, 3–4in (7.5–10cm)
   in diameter
1 ball mozzarella cheese,
   drained and sliced

### For the sauce

1 large onion, finely chopped
2 garlic cloves, crushed
1 tsp chopped rosemary
1 tsp chopped thyme
1 tsp chopped oregano
1 tsp chopped basil
2 tbsp tomato paste
14oz (400g) can chopped
   tomatoes

### For the breadcrumb mixture

⅔ cup breadcrumbs
⅓ cup all-purpose flour
1 cup grated
   Parmesan cheese
salt and freshly ground
   black pepper

**1** For the sauce, heat a little oil in a saucepan over medium heat. Add the onion and cook for 3–4 minutes. Add the garlic and the herbs. Sauté for 2–3 minutes, or until the onions have softened. Add the tomato paste and continue to stir for 2–3 minutes. Add the tomatoes with their juices. Reduce the heat and simmer for 30 minutes, or until the sauce has thickened and the flavors have mellowed.

**2** Meanwhile, preheat the oven to 350°F (180°C). In a medium bowl, mix the breadcrumbs, flour, Parmesan, and season to taste.

**3** Cut each chicken breast into four pieces, so that each piece is roughly the size of the bun. Pour the oil into a bowl, dip the breasts in it, and then coat them in the breadcrumb mixture. Place them on a baking sheet lined with parchment paper. Bake for 15–20 minutes or until crisp, turning them halfway through to ensure they are evenly cooked.

**4** Cut the buns in half. Fill each bun with 1 tbsp of tomato sauce, one piece of the baked chicken, and a thick slice of mozzarella. Brush the insides of the top halves of the buns with oil. Transfer the top halves, oiled-side up, and the sliders onto a baking sheet. Broil on very low heat for 2 minutes, or until the mozzarella melts and bubbles. Assemble the sandwiches and serve hot.

# CORNMEAL-CRUSTED CATFISH NUGGETS

These crispy, crunchy catfish bites are perfect with
a simple-to-prepare homemade tartare sauce.

★ **SERVES** 4

★ **PREP TIME** 10 mins,
plus chilling

★ **COOK TIME** 10 mins

## Ingredients

1lb 5oz (600g) catfish nuggets
or skinless firm-fleshed white
fish fillets, such as coley
2 tbsp all-purpose flour
1 egg, lightly beaten
½ cup cornmeal or fine polenta
salt and freshly ground
black pepper
peanut or sunflower oil,
for frying
potato wedges, to serve

## For the tartare sauce

2 small pickles, coarsely grated
6 heaped tbsp good-quality
mayonnaise
1 tbsp white wine vinegar
1 tbsp capers, very
finely chopped
finely grated zest of ½ lemon
1 heaped tbsp finely
chopped dill

**1** Cut the fish into ¾in- (2cm-) thick strips. Pat it dry with paper towels. Put the flour, egg, and cornmeal in 3 shallow bowls. Season the flour well.

**2** Coat the fish pieces by dusting them first with the flour, then dipping them in the egg, then rolling them in the cornmeal, until they are well covered. Put them on a plate, cover with plastic wrap, and chill for 30 minutes. This helps the coating to stick.

**3** Meanwhile, make the tartare sauce. First, put the pickles on to a chopping board and chop again, finely, with a sharp knife. Mix the pickles, mayonnaise, vinegar, capers, lemon zest, and dill, and season well. Cover and chill until needed.

**4** Heat a large, deep-sided frying pan and add enough oil to cover the base. Fry the fish pieces for 2 minutes on each side, turning carefully, until golden and crisp all over. Rest them on a plate lined with paper towels while you cook the rest. Serve with potato wedges and the tartare sauce.

**COOK'S TIP** You can also add seasonings, such as ½ tsp onion powder or 1 tsp smoked paprika, to the cornmeal, if you like.

**Dill**, an aromatic herb, is best used fresh, and is frequently paired with fish dishes.

# BLACKENED MAHI-MAHI WITH PINEAPPLE SALSA

This warm-water fish with a Hawaiian name is given a Caribbean twist with a sweet and spicy pineapple salsa.

★ **SERVES** 5
★ **COOK TIME** 20 mins
★ **PREP TIME** 4-6 mins

**Ingredients**

½ stick (4 tbsps) butter, melted
2 tsp sea salt
2 tsp garlic powder
2 tsp freshly ground black pepper
1 tsp cayenne pepper
1 tsp dried oregano
1 tsp dried thyme
5 x 5½oz (150g) mahi-mahi fillets, skins removed; or a firm, white fish, such as snapper

**For the salsa**

½ pineapple, skinned and cored (see technique, right)
1 red bell pepper, halved and seeded
1 red onion, finely chopped
1 jalapeño or other mild green chile, seeded (optional) and finely chopped
1 garlic clove, crushed
juice of 2 limes
handful of cilantro, finely chopped

**1** For the salsa, chop the pineapple and pepper into small, similar-sized chunks and put them in a bowl. Add the onion, jalapeño, garlic, lime juice, and cilantro, and stir to mix. Set aside.

**2** Pour the melted butter into a wide, shallow bowl. In another wide, shallow bowl, mix the sea salt, garlic powder, black pepper, cayenne pepper, oregano, and thyme.

**3** Heat a large, heavy-based frying pan over medium-high heat. When the pan is hot, dip the fish fillets in the melted butter, coating both sides well, then dip in the seasoning.

**4** Cook the fillets for 2–3 minutes on each side, or until blackened. Serve hot, topped with the pineapple salsa.

## CORING A PINEAPPLE

**1 With a sharp knife**, cut off the top and the base. Stand it upright and cut along the contour of the flesh, removing the skin in strips from top to bottom.

**2 Turn the pineapple sideways** and cut it into slices of an even thickness. Use a round metal cutter to remove the hard, fibrous center of each ring.

# ZESTY PASTALAYA

Try a new twist on a classic jambalaya by replacing
the customary rice with orzo, a rice-shaped pasta.

★ **SERVES** 6–8
★ **PREP TIME** 20 mins
★ **COOK TIME** 2–2½ hrs

**Ingredients**

1 tbsp olive oil
1lb 2oz (500g) skin-on,
  bone-in chicken thighs
3 garlic cloves, crushed
10oz (300g) onion, diced
1 green bell pepper, seeded
  and roughly chopped
3 celery stalks, about
  9oz (250g) in total, sliced
2 x 14oz (400g) can chopped
  tomatoes
2 bay leaves
juice of 1 lemon
3 tbsp Worcestershire sauce
1 tbsp hot sauce
1 tsp cayenne pepper
1 tsp dried oregano
salt and freshly ground
  black pepper
1lb 2oz (500g) chorizo, sliced
1 cup orzo
zest and juice of 2 lemons,
  to serve
1lb 2oz (500g) raw shrimp,
  peeled and deveined

**1** Heat the oil in a large soup pot over medium heat. Cook the chicken for 2 minutes on each side until browned. Set aside. Add the garlic, onion, pepper, and celery to the pot and cook for 4–5 minutes, or until the onions are tender.

**2** Return the chicken to the pot and cover with 4¼ cups of water. Add the tomatoes, bay leaves, lemon juice, Worcestershire sauce, hot sauce, and spices. Season to taste and bring to a boil.

**3** Meanwhile, in a frying pan, cook the chorizo for 3–5 minutes, or until browned. Add it to the pot. Reduce the heat to a simmer and cook, uncovered, for 1½–2 hours.

**4** In a saucepan, cook the orzo in 3¼ cups of water with the lid slightly open for 10–12 minutes, or until tender. Drain and toss with lemon juice.

**5** When the chicken is falling off the bone, remove it from the pot using a slotted spoon and transfer to a plate. Discard the skin and shred the chicken using a fork. Discard the bones and return the chicken meat to the pot. Add the shrimp, cooking for 5–7 minutes, or until pink.

**6** Stir in the orzo, season to taste, and remove the bay leaves. Serve hot, topped with a pinch of lemon zest and a squeeze of lemon.

# BROWN ALE CIOPPINO

Traditionally made with the seafood catch of the day, cioppino can be adapted to use whatever fish or shellfish is available.

★ **SERVES** 6
★ **PREP TIME** 20 mins
★ **COOK TIME** 55 mins

### Ingredients

1 tbsp butter
1 tbsp olive oil
2 garlic cloves, crushed
1 onion, roughly chopped
2 shallots, sliced
1 celery stalk, including
    greens, sliced
⅔ cup tomato paste
salt and freshly ground
    black pepper
1 tsp red pepper flakes
2 x 14oz (400g) can chopped
    tomatoes
1 cup dry white wine
4¼ cups hot fish stock
1½ cups brown ale
6–12 top neck clams, fresh
    in shells
6–12 mussels, fresh in shells
6oz (175g) salmon fillet, cut
    into bite-sized pieces
1lb (450g) large shrimp, heads
    on, peeled, and deveined
crusty bread, to serve

**1** In a large, heavy-based pan, heat the butter and oil over medium heat and add the garlic, onion, shallots, and celery. Cook, stirring occasionally, for 5–7 minutes. Stir in the tomato paste, season with salt and pepper and the red pepper flakes, and cook, stirring, for 1–2 minutes.

**2** Add the tomatoes with their juices, wine, stock, and ale. Stir to incorporate. Reduce the heat to a simmer and cook for 35 minutes.

**3** Scrub the clams and mussels, discarding any that stay open when tapped. Add them to the pot and simmer for 5 minutes, or until they open. Discard any that do not open.

**4** Stir in the salmon and shrimp, and simmer for a further 5 minutes, or until the shrimp are pink and the salmon is cooked through. Season to taste and serve hot with crusty bread.

# SWEET AND SMOKY SHRIMP AND GRITS

This popular Southern dish of creamy grits is paired with a sweet, salty, and smoky topping of shrimp and bacon.

★ **SERVES** 4
★ **PREP TIME** 15 mins
★ **COOK TIME** 1 hr

### Ingredients

4 thick-cut smoked bacon slices
2 garlic cloves, crushed
1 onion, roughly chopped
4 large tomatoes,
    roughly chopped
6 tbsps butter
1 tbsp light brown sugar
1 tsp red pepper flakes
salt and freshly ground
    black pepper
2 cups yellow grits or polenta
2 cups heavy cream or
    whole milk
¼ tsp smoked paprika
    or ancho chilli powder
¼ tsp cayenne pepper
2 cups cheddar cheese, grated
juice of 1 lemon
1lb (450g) raw shrimp,
    shelled and deveined
2 scallions, chopped, to garnish

**1** In a heavy-based frying pan, dry-fry the bacon, drain on paper towels, and set aside. Drain off most of the bacon grease from the pan and return to medium-low heat. Add the garlic, onion, tomatoes, butter, sugar, red pepper flakes, and season well. Cook over low heat, stirring occasionally, for 30–45 minutes, or until the onion and tomatoes have softened.

**2** After simmering the tomato mixture for 15 minutes, combine the grits, cream, 1¾ pints (1 liter) of water, smoked paprika, and cayenne pepper in a large soup pot, and season well. Cook over medium-low heat for 30–35 minutes, or until the grits thicken and can hold a spoon on the surface, and about three-quarters of the liquid has been absorbed. Stir in the cheese until melted and fully incorporated, then add the lemon juice.

**3** Add the shrimp to the tomato mixture in the frying pan and cook for 5–7 minutes, or until the shrimp turn pink. Crumble or chop the bacon.

**4** Transfer the grits to a serving dish and top with the tomato and shrimp sauce, crumbled bacon, and scallions. Serve hot.

**COOK'S TIP** For a lighter take on creamy grits, try almond milk instead of heavy cream or whole milk.

# CAJUN ANDOUILLE GUMBO

Rustic Cajun-style cooking is often a one-pot affair, and this hearty gumbo is a perfect example.

★ **SERVES** 4
★ **PREP TIME** 15 mins
★ **COOK TIME** 1 hr

### Ingredients

2 tbsp olive oil
1 large onion, finely chopped
1 green pepper, seeded and
 cut into ¾in (2cm) cubes
2 garlic cloves, crushed
2 tbsp unsalted butter
¼ cup all-purpose flour
2 x 14oz (400g) can
 chopped tomatoes
2 cups hot fish or chicken
 stock
2 dried red chiles,
 finely chopped
1 tsp smoked paprika
 or ancho chili powder
7oz (200g) okra, trimmed and
 cut into ¾in (2cm) chunks
9oz (250g) andouille
 smoked sausage,
 peeled and cut into
 ¾in (2cm) chunks
salt and freshly ground
 black pepper
1 tbsp thyme leaves
1lb 2oz (500g) raw
 large shrimp, shelled
 and deveined
2 tbsp finely chopped
 flat-leaf parsley
boiled rice, to serve

**1** Heat the oil in a large, heavy-based saucepan. Add the onion and green pepper, and cook gently for 5 minutes until soft, but not brown. Add the garlic and cook for a further 2 minutes.

**2** Add the butter to the pan and allow it to melt, then add the flour and stir on a very low heat for 5 minutes, until browned. Add the tomatoes, stock, chiles, paprika, okra, and sausage, and bring to a boil. Taste and season with pepper, and salt if necessary (the stock may be salty).

**3** Reduce the heat to a low simmer and add the thyme. Cook, uncovered, for 30 minutes, stirring occasionally, until the okra is soft and the gumbo well thickened.

**4** Increase the heat and add the shrimp. Cook the gumbo, uncovered, for a further 5 minutes, until the shrimp are opaque and cooked through. Stir through the parsley and serve with rice.

**COOK'S TIP** If you can't get hold of andouille sausage, you can substitute it with smoked chorizo or kiełbasa.

# NOW TRY...

## CATFISH

Replace the sausage with 1lb (450g) **catfish** chunks (or other firm-fleshed white fish) and add them along with the shrimp in step 4. Cook gently until the fish is opaque, stirring only occasionally.

## CHICKEN & PANCETTA

Replace the shrimp with 1lb 5oz (600g) skinless and boneless **chicken thighs**, cut into 1¼in (3cm) chunks, and replace the sausage with the same amount of **diced pancetta**. Add the chicken at the end of step 1, and brown it with the vegetables before continuing as usual.

## VEGETARIAN

Remove the sausage and the shrimp. Add 1 **eggplant**, cut into ½in (1cm) chunks, along with the green peppers in step 1. Add 2 large **sweet potatoes**, peeled and cut into ½in (1cm) chunks, 10 minutes before the end of cooking time in step 3, or until the potato is just soft, before serving over rice.

# SPICY CHORIZO-STYLE DIRTY RICE

This Cajun dish traditionally uses chicken gizzards to give the rice a "dirty" appearance. Here, chicken livers do the job just as well.

★ **SERVES** 4-6
★ **PREP TIME** 15 mins
★ **COOK TIME** 1 hr, plus resting

### Ingredients

¼ cup olive oil
1 onion, finely chopped
1 celery stalk, trimmed
  and finely sliced
1 red bell pepper, seeded and
  cut into ½in (1cm) cubes
1 green bell pepper, seeded and
  cut into ½in (1cm) cubes
14oz (400g) spicy chorizo-style
  sausage, skinned
7oz (200g) chicken livers,
  cleaned, trimmed, and
  finely chopped
1 red chile, seeded and
  finely chopped
2 garlic cloves, finely chopped
1 tsp smoked paprika or ancho
  chili powder
1 tsp coriander seeds, crushed
1⅔ cups long-grain rice
salt and freshly ground
  black pepper
3¼ cups hot chicken stock
leaves from 1 large sprig
  of thyme
handful of flat-leaf parsley,
  finely chopped
1 tbsp finely chopped oregano
mixed leaf salad, to serve
crusty bread, to serve

**1** Preheat the oven to 325°F (160°C). Heat 3 tbsp of oil in a large, cast-iron, flameproof casserole, and add the onion, celery, and peppers. Cook over low heat for 5–7 minutes, until softened. Remove the vegetables and set aside.

**2** Add the remaining oil to the casserole, then crumble the sausage meat into the pan, along with the chicken livers. Increase the heat and cook for 5 minutes, until the sausage meat is broken up, seared, and no longer pink.

**3** Add the chile, garlic, paprika, and coriander seeds, and cook for a further 2–3 minutes. Return the vegetables to the casserole, then stir in the rice. Season well, and add the stock.

**4** Bring to a boil, cover, and transfer to the oven. Cook for up to 40 minutes, stirring once or twice, until the rice is cooked and the stock has been absorbed. Remove from the oven and rest for 5 minutes. Stir in the herbs, check the seasoning, and serve with a mixed leaf salad and crusty bread.

**Chorizo** can be bought fresh, cured, or dried. Softer chorizo is better for cooking.

# SEARED TUNA AND CREAMY LIMA BEAN PASTA

Fresh tuna and creamy lima beans give that classic dish, tuna casserole, a sophisticated twist.

★ **SERVES** 4
★ **PREP TIME** 10 mins
★ **COOK TIME** 30 mins

## Ingredients

1 tbsp olive oil
4 tuna steaks, about
   12oz (350g) in total
salt and freshly ground
   black pepper
1lb (450g) thin spaghetti,
   such as angel hair

## For the sauce

1 cup heavy cream
1 tbsp all-purpose flour
2 tbsp butter
juice of 1 lemon
salt and freshly ground
   black pepper
14oz (400g) can lima beans

**1** First, make the sauce. In a saucepan, combine the cream, flour, butter, lemon juice, and seasoning over medium heat. Bring to a boil, then reduce the heat to a simmer and cook for 10–15 minutes. Stir in the beans and simmer for a further 5 minutes.

**2** Meanwhile, heat the oil in a heavy-based frying pan over high heat. Sprinkle both sides of the tuna steaks with salt and pepper. Cook each steak for 2–3 minutes on each side—the tuna should remain pink in the middle.

**3** Boil the spaghetti in a saucepan of salted water until tender, or according to the package instructions. Drain well and toss the pasta in the bean sauce and divide between 4 plates. Cut the tuna into thick slices and serve hot on a bed of spaghetti.

# A taste of the
# SOUTHWEST

Southwestern cooking, with its fresh, vibrant flavors and strong, bold colors, evolved out of a happy marriage of Spanish, Native American, and Mexican cuisines.

## FOODS AND FLAVORS

★ **Corn**, in all its incarnations, is considered a sacred food by the Native Americans; before the arrival of European settlers, more than 40 varieties were cultivated.

★ **Dried beans**, usually black or pinto beans, are a major feature of the cuisine, and are typically slow-cooked, baked, or refried (see below).

★ **Chilies**, whether red or green, hot or mild, are the primary source of heat in the region's best-known dish–chili (or chili con carne)– which can be red, green, or white.

★ **Tortillas**, now available made of either corn or wheat, were originally made only of ground corn–using yellow, white, or the unusual blue corn of the area.

★ **Navajo fry bread**, a simple flat bread prepared on an iron skillet, is similar in style to the ubiquitous Mexican tortilla.

The mainstays of the Southwestern diet are rice and tomatoes—both of which were introduced by Spanish settlers—corn, a variety of dried beans, fresh cilantro, and the ever-present chile peppers that appear in many of the region's dishes. Beef and pork are the main meats eaten here.

Southwestern cuisine combines a mixture of cooking styles belonging to the various groups of people who came to live in the region, which was settled early by Spanish colonists traveling north from Mexico, and who learned to cook alongside their Native American neighbors. Today, both quick, fierce heat and long, slow cooking methods are used to prepare a variety of dishes, from stews rich with tomatoes and spices, to grilled marinated beef ("carne asada"), which is sliced paper thin for topping tacos laden with herbs. Unusual vegetables, such as jícama, tomatillos (see above), and nopales— the peeled pads of the prickly pear cactus—all grow well in the dry heat, and feature in many local dishes.

**When preserving chilies for the coming year, tradition dictates that strings equal to the height of each family member should be made to ensure a good supply until the next harvest.**

Chipotle chiles are smoked, dried jalepeño chiles, and are used widely in the cuisine of the southwest.

A new take on a classic Mexican dish, the breakfast burrito can be as varied as you like.

Some purists insist that chili be made with meat only, but for many, beans are an essential addition.

HISTORIC
NEW MEXICO
U.S.
66
ROUTE

Enchiladas, a type of stuffed and baked tortilla wrap, lend themselves well to a variety of fillings.

The southwest boasts some of the most dramatic landscapes in the country.

Strings of chilies, known as "ristras," are a decorative way of preserving chilies for several months.

# COUNTRY FRIED STEAK WITH PEPPER GRAVY

Also known as "chicken fried steak" for its similarity to fried chicken, this Southern dish is home cooking at its best.

★ **SERVES** 4
★ **PREP TIME** 15 mins, plus soaking
★ **COOK TIME** 35 mins

### Ingredients

4 x 5½oz (150g) tenderized rump or sirloin steaks, whole
1 cup whole milk
salt and freshly ground black pepper
1 tsp cayenne pepper
1 egg
1¾ cups all-purpose flour
½ cup peanut or sunflower oil, for frying

### For the gravy

¼ cup all-purpose flour
2 cups whole milk

### For the home fries

2¼lb (1kg) potatoes, such as Russet
4 slices smoked bacon
1 onion, chopped
2 garlic cloves, crushed
pinch of red pepper flakes

**1** Soak the steaks overnight in milk with salt and black pepper, and a pinch of cayenne pepper. The following day, take out the steaks and set aside. Beat the egg into the milk in a small bowl. In a separate bowl, combine the flour with salt and black pepper, and the remaining cayenne pepper.

**2** In a frying pan, heat the oil until hot. Toss each steak in the flour, then dip into the milk mixture, and again in the flour. Fry for 3–5 minutes on each side, or until golden brown and cooked through. Watch the meat carefully so that it does not burn.

**3** Once the meat is cooked, remove from the pan and set aside. Drain two-thirds of the oil. For the gravy, add the flour to the remaining oil in the pan and whisk to a thick paste. Slowly add the milk, 1 cup at a time, stirring constantly. Once a thick gravy has formed, remove from the heat and season generously with black pepper.

**4** For the home fries, cook the potatoes in a pan of boiling water for 20 minutes. Drain the potatoes and set aside to cool. When cool enough to handle, leaving the skins on, cut the potatoes into ¾in (2cm) strips.

**5** In a large, nonstick frying pan, dry-fry the bacon until crisp. Crumble the bacon and add the potatoes along with the onion, garlic, and red pepper flakes. Season to taste. Cook over medium heat until crisp. Serve the steaks with a generous portion of the gravy and home fries on the side.

# SPAGHETTI AND HERBED TURKEY MEATBALLS

Ground turkey makes a healthy, low-fat alternative to ground beef in this popular family dish.

★ **SERVES** 4
★ **PREP TIME** 20 mins
★ **COOK TIME** 1 hr 10 mins

### Ingredients
olive oil, for cooking and
    drizzling
1lb (450g) dried spaghetti

**For the sauce**
3 garlic cloves, crushed
1 onion, chopped
1 tsp dried rosemary
1 tsp dried oregano
1 tsp dried thyme
2 tbsp tomato paste
2 x 15oz (400g) can chopped
    tomatoes

**For the meatballs**
1lb (450g) turkey, ground
1 cup breadcrumbs
1 shallot, sliced
bunch of basil, chopped
1 egg, beaten
salt and freshly ground
    black pepper

**1** First, make the sauce. Heat a little oil in a saucepan over medium heat. Sauté the garlic and onion briefly, then add the rosemary, oregano, and thyme. Cook for 2–3 minutes, or until the onion has softened slightly. Stir in the tomato paste, then add the chopped tomatoes with their juices. Reduce the heat and simmer to thicken for 1 hour.

**2** Meanwhile, preheat the oven to 350°F (180°C). For the meatballs, mix the turkey, breadcrumbs, shallot, basil, egg, and seasoning in a bowl. Using your hands, form the mixture into twelve 2in (5cm) balls and place them on a baking sheet lined with parchment paper.

**3** Bake for 35–40 minutes, or until browned, sizzling, and cooked through. Remove from the oven and put them into the simmering sauce, stirring to incorporate.

**4** Cook the pasta in a large pan of boiling salted water for 8–10 minutes, or according to package instructions. Drain, drizzle over a little oil, and toss well. Serve the spaghetti hot, topped with a generous portion of the sauce and meatballs.

# THREE BEAN CHILI

A big pot of chili is an easy way to make a little meat go a long way.

- ★ **SERVES** 4-6
- ★ **PREP TIME** 10 mins
- ★ **COOK TIME** 2 hrs

### Ingredients

1 green bell pepper, seeded and roughly chopped
1 red bell pepper, seeded and roughly chopped
1 onion, roughly chopped
1 jalapeño or other mild green chile, roughly chopped
2 tbsp olive oil
2 x 15oz (425g) can chopped tomatoes
12oz (340g) can corn, drained
140z (400g) can each of red kidney beans, black beans, and cannellini beans
3 garlic cloves, finely chopped
1lb (450g) ground beef
½ tbsp salt and ½ tsp freshly ground black pepper
1 tsp red pepper flakes
1 tbsp chili powder
1 tbsp ground cumin

### To serve

Southern-style cornbread (see p228)
grated cheddar cheese
sour cream

**1** Combine the peppers, onion, and jalapeño in a Dutch oven or large flameproof casserole with a drizzle of oil. Add the tomatoes, corn, and beans. Stir well to incorporate.

**2** In a heavy-based frying pan, heat the remaining oil over medium heat. Add the garlic and fry for 1 minute, then add the beef and cook, stirring occasionally, for 3–4 minutes, or until browned all over. Transfer to the casserole, season with the salt and pepper, and add the spices.

**3** Place the uncovered casserole over low heat and simmer for 2 hours, stirring occasionally, or until the vegetables are tender. Alternatively, place the dish in an oven preheated at 350°F (180°C). Season to taste. Serve hot with cornbread, cheddar cheese, and sour cream.

★★★
### WHAT'S THE STORY?

The official state dish of Texas, chili (also known as chilli con carne) was popular with the American frontier settlers of the 19th century. Today, there is much debate about whether it should be made with or without beans. Some purists insist on a simple combination of onions, tomatoes, chilies, spices, and meat, but more often canned or dried beans are added too.

★★★

## NOW TRY...

### WHITE CHILI

Brown 2 diced **chicken breasts** and add 14oz can each of **cannellini beans** and garbanzo **beans**, drained; 2 sliced **shallots**; 3 garlic **cloves**; 3 cups **hot chicken stock**; and the spices and seasoning from the main recipe. Simmer, uncovered, for 2–3 hours until the liquid reduces to a thick sauce.

### VEGGIE OPTION

Substitute the meat with ½ cup **bulgur wheat** for a hearty vegetarian chili. Add to step 1 along with the garlic, seasoning, and spices and skip step 2.

### FIVE ALARM CHILI

In step 1, add 2 **red peppers**, another **jalapeño** or other mild green chile, and stir in ½ tbsp **cayenne pepper**, ½ tbsp **chipotle paste**, and ½ tbsp **smoked paprika** or ancho chili powder. Cook as per the main recipe and serve with chopped **cilantro** and diced **avocado**.

# SWEET AND SPICY MEATLOAF

Sweet pepper jelly makes a tasty alternative to the traditional ketchup topping for this classic family dish.

★ **SERVES** 6
★ **PREP TIME** 15 mins
★ **COOK TIME** 1 hr

## Ingredients

1lb (450g) ground beef
1 onion, chopped
⅔ cup panko breadcrumbs
  or day-old breadcrumbs
3 garlic cloves, crushed
1 tsp red pepper flakes
1 tsp chipotle paste
salt and freshly ground
  black pepper
1 egg, beaten
4 tbsp Hot pepper jelly
  (see p248)
mashed potatoes (see p156),
  to serve

**1** Preheat the oven to 350°F (180°C). In a large bowl, combine the meat, onion, breadcrumbs, garlic, red pepper flakes, and chipotle paste, and season well. Add the egg and, using your hands or a large spoon, mix all the ingredients together until well combined. Shape the meat mixture into a loosely formed ball.

**2** Line a baking sheet with parchment paper and transfer the meatball to the baking sheet. Using your hands, mold the meatball into a rectangular loaf. Top generously with hot pepper jelly and bake for 1 hour, or until a thermometer inserted into the meat reads 170°F (77°C).

**3** Slice the loaf with a sharp, serrated knife and serve hot with mashed potatoes and additional pepper jelly on the side.

**Red pepper flakes** often include the spicy seeds, so use sparingly if you don't like your food too hot.

# SPICY GRILLED BRISKET

Cooking the brisket long and slow, wrapped in foil to preserve the juices, means the meat will be tender and falling apart.

★ **SERVES** 6-8

★ **PREP TIME** 5 mins, plus chilling

★ **COOK TIME** 4-5 hrs, plus resting

### Ingredients

1 tsp cayenne pepper

1 tsp garlic powder

1 tsp oregano

1 tsp black pepper

2 tbsp ground coffee

1 tsp chipotle paste

1 tsp peanut or sunflower oil

1 tbsp sea salt

beef brisket, about 5lb (2.25kg)

grilled corn (see p153) or potato salad (see p50), to serve

**1** The night before you plan to cook the brisket, mix together the cayenne pepper, garlic, oregano, black pepper, coffee, chipotle paste, oil, and sea salt. Rub this mixture evenly across all sides of the brisket. Wrap the beef with foil and let it chill overnight.

**2** On the top rack of a gas grill, cook the brisket in the foil for 4–5 hours at 250–300°F (130–150°C), with the lid closed. Alternatively, cook in the oven at 300°F (150°C) for 4–5 hours, or until a thermometer inserted into the meat reads 195°F (90°C). Remove from the heat and let it rest, covered in foil and its juices, for 1 hour. Slice and serve warm with grilled corn and potato salad.

**COOK'S TIP** For a smoky flavor, add a pan of hickory chips tossed in 1 cup of water to the grill.

# SLOW-COOKED POT ROAST

This rich dish is cooked long and slow, until the meat almost falls apart, and is served with buttery egg noodles.

★ **SERVES** 4
★ **PREP TIME** 20 mins
★ **COOK TIME** 4 hrs

**Ingredients**

6 tbsps butter, softened
3 garlic cloves, finely chopped
2lb (900g) topside or chuck roast
1 onion, roughly chopped
12 cremini or button mushrooms, halved
2 beets, roughly chopped
2 carrots, roughly chopped
2 yellow or gold potatoes, cut into cubes
1 sweet potato, peeled and roughly chopped
1 bay leaf, finely chopped
1 tbsp chopped rosemary
1 tbsp chopped oregano
1 tbsp chopped thyme
1 cup hot chicken stock
1 cup red wine
salt and freshly ground black pepper
9oz (250g) dried egg noodles

**1** In a Dutch oven or flameproof casserole, melt 2 tbsp of the butter and sauté the garlic over medium heat for 1–2 minutes. Add the meat and cook for 1 minute on each side to brown. Remove the meat and set aside.

**2** Add the onion and mushrooms to the casserole and cook for 2–3 minutes. Then add another 2 tbsp butter, the beets, carrots, potatoes, and sweet potato, and stir in the herbs. Add the stock and wine, and season well.

**3** Return the meat to the casserole, nestling it on top of the root vegetables. Cover and simmer, checking and stirring occasionally, for 3½–4 hours, or until the meat is tender. Remove the meat and cut it into thick slices; it should fall apart easily. Strain the gravy into a pitcher.

**4** Cook the noodles in a saucepan of salted boiling water until soft, or according to the instructions on the package. Drain and toss with the remaining butter. Lay out the vegetables on a serving plate and top with the sliced meat. Serve hot with the noodles and the gravy.

**Beets** have an earthy, sweet taste, perfect for this warming, wintry dish.

# CLASSIC BURGERS

Using very lean meat can make the burger dry. A little fat keeps the meat juicy, basting it from within.

★ **SERVES** 4
★ **PREP TIME** 20 mins, plus chilling
★ **COOK TIME** 10 mins

### Ingredients
14oz (400g) good-quality
   ground beef
½ cup fresh white
   breadcrumbs
1 egg yolk
½ red onion, finely chopped
½ tsp dried mustard powder
½ tsp celery salt
1 tsp Worcestershire sauce
freshly ground black pepper

### To serve
4 burger buns, halved
1 head lettuce, shredded
2 tomatoes, thickly sliced
1 small red onion,
   finely sliced
1 pickle, finely sliced
¼ cup No-cook spicy
   summer relish
   (see p244)

**1** Prepare a grill for cooking. In a large bowl, mix together all the burger ingredients until well combined.

**2** With damp hands (to help stop the mixture sticking to your fingers), divide the mixture into 4 balls and roll each between your palms until smooth. Flatten each ball out into a large, fat disk to a thickness of 1¼in (3cm), and pat the edges in to tidy them up.

**3** Place the burgers on a plate, cover with plastic wrap, and chill for 30 minutes (this will help them to keep their shape during cooking).

**4** Cook over a hot grill for 6–8 minutes, turning as needed, until the meat is springy to the touch and the edges charred. While the hamburgers are grilling, grill the buns for 1–2 minutes on the insides only, until lightly charred. Serve the burgers and buns with a selection of accompaniments, and let everyone assemble their own burgers as they prefer.

## NOW TRY...

### MOROCCAN STYLE

Replace the beef with **ground lamb**, and the spices with ¼ cup finely chopped **mint leaves**, ½ tsp **ground cinnamon**, and ½ tsp **ground cumin**. Serve inside warm **pita bread** with a spoonful of **minted Greek yogurt**.

### ASIAN TWIST

For a leaner burger, replace the beef with **ground chicken** or **turkey**, and the spices with 1 **red chile**, finely chopped, 1¼in (3cm) of fresh grated **ginger**, finely chopped, and ¼ cup finely chopped **cilantro**. Serve with **sour cream** and Thai **sweet chili sauce**.

### PATTY MELT

Follow the recipe for the Grilled cheese sandwich on p90 but use a **rustic loaf** and add some store-bought **caramelized onions** and a **grilled burger** to the cheesy filling (making sure the sandwich starts and finishes with a layer of grated cheese).

# DRY-RUB STEAK WITH CHIMICHURRI SAUCE

Crusty on the outside and juicy on the inside, this sweet, spicy steak pairs beautifully with the fresh and piquant sauce.

★ **SERVES** 4

★ **PREP TIME** 15 mins, plus minimum 1 hr resting

★ **COOK TIME** 8–20 mins, plus resting

### Ingredients

1 flank or skirt steak, about 1½ lb (675g)

### For the dry rub

1 tbsp light brown sugar

1 tbsp thyme leaves

½ tsp dried mustard powder

¼ tsp garlic salt

¼ tsp smoked paprika or ancho chile powder

freshly ground black pepper

### For the chimichurri sauce

6 tbsp olive oil, plus extra for brushing

1½ tbsp red wine vinegar

1 tbsp lemon juice

handful of flat-leaf parsley leaves, about 1 tbsp

2 tbsp chopped cilantro leaves

1 tbsp chopped oregano leaves

2 garlic cloves, chopped

1 tsp dried red chile flakes

salt and freshly ground black pepper

**1** In the small bowl of a food processor, grind all the ingredients for the dry rub together to form a fine powder.

**2** Place the steak on a large piece of plastic wrap and rub half of the mixture into each side. Wrap it tightly in the plastic wrap and chill for at least 1 hour.

**3** Place all the ingredients for the chimichurri sauce in a blender, or the small bowl of a food processor, and process to a thick, emulsified green sauce. Place in a serving bowl, cover in plastic wrap, and chill for at least 1 hour, to allow the flavors to develop.

**4** When you are ready to cook, take the steak and the sauce out of the fridge and allow them to come to room temperature. Brush the steak with a little oil, and grill for 4–10 minutes on each side, depending on how you like your meat. For rare, allow 4–6 minutes on each side; for medium, 6–8 minutes; and for well done, 8–10 minutes.

**5** Remove from the heat and allow the meat to rest, covered lightly in foil, for at least 10 minutes before slicing and serving with the chimichurri sauce.

# SLOW-COOKED PULLED PORK WRAPS

Here, the pork is cooked until it is juicy and falls apart easily, then it is shredded and smothered in delicious sauce.

★ **SERVES** 6-8
★ **PREP TIME** 30 mins, plus marinating
★ **COOK TIME** 3 hrs, plus resting

### Ingredients
4½lb (2kg) bone-in pork shoulder
salt, for rubbing

### For the marinade
2 tbsp peanut or sunflower oil, plus extra for rubbing
1 onion, finely chopped
2 garlic cloves, crushed
½ cup ketchup
¼ cup apple cider vinegar
1 tsp Tabasco or other hot sauce
1 tsp Worcestershire sauce
1 tsp dried mustard powder
2 tbsp honey

### To serve
selection of tortilla wraps
sour cream
peach salsa (see p10) or salsa verde (see p79)
guacamole (see p11)
lettuce
finely sliced red onions

**1** To make the marinade, heat the oil in a small, heavy-based pan. Cook the onion over medium heat for 5 minutes until softened. Add the garlic and cook for 1 minute. Add the remaining ingredients along with ½ cup of water, and whisk well.

**2** Bring to a boil, reduce the heat to a simmer, and cook, uncovered, for 20 minutes until reduced to a thick sauce. Use a hand-held blender or food processor to blend it until smooth. Leave to cool. Rub the pork with the marinade, then place in a large, shallow dish. Cover and marinate in the fridge for at least 4 hours, but preferably overnight.

**3** Preheat the oven to 350°F (180°C). Put the pork and marinade in a baking pan just big enough to fit it. Put a piece of parchment paper over the top (to stop the skin sticking to the foil) and seal with a double layer of foil. Cook the pork for 2½ hours.

**4** Prepare a grill for grilling. Remove the meat from the oven. Pat the skin dry with paper towels and rub in a little oil, then some salt. Cook it over the hot grill for 10–15 minutes on each side, skin-side down first; carefully turn with tongs, but do not turn it until the skin is crispy and charred in places.

**5** Meanwhile, pour the juices from the oven sheet into a saucepan and first pour, then skim off all the fat. Reduce the sauce over medium heat to a thick pouring consistency.

**6** Cut the skin off the meat and leave it uncovered (or it will go soft) while you rest the meat, wrapped in foil, for 10 minutes. When ready to serve, cut the crispy skin into shards. Shred the pork into a juicy pile, pour over the sauce, and serve with the wraps and accompaniments.

# STOVETOP BRUNSWICK STEW

The county of Brunswick, Virginia, and Brunswick, Georgia, both claim this thick, tomato-based stew as their own.

★ **SERVES** 6-8
★ **PREP TIME** 15 mins
★ **COOK TIME** 3 hrs

### Ingredients

1 tbsp butter
1¾lb (800g) skin-on, bone-in
  chicken thighs
12oz (350g) bone-in pork loin
2 garlic cloves, crushed
10oz (300g) onion, diced
3½oz (100g) celery stalks, sliced
9oz (250g) white potatoes,
  skin on, chopped
12oz (340g) can corn, with
  its juices
14oz (400g) can lima beans,
  with their juices
2 x 14oz (400g) can chopped
  tomatoes, with their juices
1 tsp red pepper flakes
2 tbsp Worcestershire sauce
salt and freshly ground
  black pepper

**1** In a large soup pot, heat the butter and brown the chicken and pork over medium heat for 1–2 minutes on each side. Remove from the pot and set aside.

**2** Add the garlic, onion, celery, and potatoes to the pot and sauté for 4–5 minutes, or until the onions soften. Stir in the corn, beans, tomatoes, red pepper flakes, and Worcestershire sauce. Return the meat to the pot and stir well.

**3** Add 1 cup of water. Bring to a boil, reduce the heat, and simmer, uncovered, for 3 hours. Remove the meat from the pot with a slotted spoon and transfer to a plate. Discard the chicken skin and shred the meat using a fork. Discard the bones and return the meat to the stew. Season to taste and serve hot.

# MOLE SHREDDED PORK ENCHILADAS

Mole is a traditional Mexican sauce flavored with chile and a little dark chocolate for a deep, rich flavor.

★ **SERVES** 4
★ **PREP TIME** 20 mins
★ **COOK TIME** 1½ hrs

### Ingredients
2lb (900g) pork tenderloin or filet
1 cup grated Cheddar or Monterey Jack cheese
4 large tortillas

### For the mole sauce
1 tsp olive oil
1 onion, finely chopped
3 garlic cloves, crushed
2 tbsp semisweet or dark chocolate
2 x 15oz (400g) can chopped tomatoes
1 tsp chipotle paste
pinch of cayenne pepper
pinch of ground cinnamon
pinch of sugar
salt and freshly ground black pepper

**1** For the mole sauce, heat the oil in a large saucepan over medium heat. Add the onion and sauté for 4 minutes until soft, then add the garlic and sauté for a further minute. Stir in the chocolate, tomatoes, chipotle, cayenne pepper, cinnamon, and sugar. Season well. Reduce the heat to a simmer.

**2** In a frying pan, seal the pork for about 30 seconds on each side over high heat. Transfer the pork to the saucepan containing the mole sauce, turning once to coat. Simmer the meat in the sauce for 1 hour, stirring occasionally. Remove the pork from the sauce and pull the meat apart with a fork.

**3** Preheat the oven to 350°F (180°C). Divide the meat and half the cheese between the 4 tortillas. Roll up the tortillas tightly.

**4** Spoon half the mole sauce into a large flameproof casserole or baking dish. Lay the stuffed tortillas, seam-side down, in a row over the sauce. Top them with the remaining sauce and cheese and bake for 25 minutes. Serve hot alongside the Refried black beans with pico de gallo from p166.

**Dark chocolate** can be used to enhance savory dishes, as it's not too sweet. Use good-quality chocolate (at least 70 percent cocoa solid).

# TWICE-COOKED BABY BACK RIBS

Slow-cooking these ribs in foil in a low oven effectively steams them, so they become melt-in-the-mouth tender.

★ **SERVES** 4
★ **PREP TIME** 30 mins, plus marinating
★ **COOK TIME** 2½ hrs

### Ingredients
1 rack of baby back ribs, about 2¼lb (1kg)

**For the dry rub**
2 tbsp light brown sugar
2 tsp smoked paprika or ancho chili powder
1 tsp dried mustard powder
½ tsp ground cumin
½ tsp celery salt
½ tsp garlic salt
½ tsp freshly ground black pepper

**For the barbecue sauce**
¼ cup peanut or sunflower oil
1 small onion, finely diced
2 garlic cloves, crushed
4 tbsp apple juice
3 tbsp ketchup
2 tbsp apple cider vinegar
1 heaped tbsp dark brown sugar
1 tbsp honey
2 tsp hot sauce
1 tsp Worcestershire sauce
1 heaped tsp mustard
1 tsp smoked paprika or ancho chili powder
¼ tsp celery salt
¼ tsp allspice
salt and freshly ground black pepper

**1** Mix all the ingredients for the dry rub together in a small bowl. Rinse the ribs and then pat them dry with paper towels. Place the ribs on a large piece of strong foil and rub one-third of the dry rub mixture on the bony side, and the remaining two-thirds on the more fleshy side of the ribs. Rub the spices in really well, then wrap the ribs tightly in the foil, making sure that they are completely sealed in. Chill for 1 hour.

**2** Preheat the oven to 300°F (150°C). Place the wrapped ribs on a large baking sheet and cook, fleshy-side up (so that they arch slightly away from the sheet) for 2 hours.

**3** For the barbecue sauce, heat the oil in a small, heavy-based saucepan and cook the onion over medium heat for about 5 minutes, until softened but not browned. Add the garlic and cook for a further 2 minutes. Add the remaining ingredients, along with 4 tbsp of water, whisk them together, and bring to a boil. Reduce the heat to a low simmer and cook, uncovered, for 15 minutes, until thickened and reduced. Blend the sauce until smooth, either in a blender or in the pan using a hand-held blender. Pour half into a bowl to use for brushing the ribs and reserve the other side for serving.

**4** Preheat the grill. When the ribs are cooked, remove them from the oven and unwrap them, being careful of any steam and hot liquid that may escape. Place them, fleshy-side down, on a board and brush the top liberally with the barbecue sauce. Cook them, bony-side down, over the hot coals, while brushing the fleshy side with more of the sauce.

**5** Turn them carefully once the underside is dark brown and crispy (about 5 minutes, depending on the heat of the grill), and cook the other side for a further 5 minutes. Serve on a board, chopped into individual ribs, with the extra barbecue sauce on the side.

**COOK'S TIP** Prepare the meat up to 2 days in advance, then finish off on the grill when ready to eat, so long as it is cooked through.

# PINEAPPLE-GLAZED BAKED HAM

A whole ham is a good choice for feeding a crowd, and the sweet and sour glaze adds flavor and color to the finished dish.

★ **SERVES** 8-10
★ **PREP TIME** 20 mins
★ **COOK TIME** 2½ hrs

**Ingredients**
4½lb (2kg) piece of
   smoked ham

**For the glaze**
3 heaped tbsp pineapple jam
2 tbsp pineapple juice
1 tbsp honey
1 heaped tbsp light brown sugar
2 tbsp whole-grain mustard
salt and freshly ground
   black pepper

**1** Preheat the oven to 325°F (160°C). Put the ham, skin-side up, on a rack inside a large roasting pan, and pour water to a depth of 1in (2.5cm) into the pan. Cover tightly with foil, making sure it is well sealed so that no steam escapes. Cook for 2 hours.

**2** Meanwhile, mix all the glaze ingredients together in a saucepan and bring to a boil. Reduce to a simmer and cook for 5–7 minutes, until thick.

**3** Remove the ham from the oven and increase the temperature to 400°F (200°C). Remove the skin (leaving a thin layer of the fat), cut a criss-cross pattern in the fat, and baste with some of the glaze, as shown below.

**4** Pour away the water in the pan and return the ham to the oven for 30 minutes, brushing with glaze every 10 minutes until browned and crispy. Serve hot with Rainbow potato gratin (see p158) and Green bean casserole (see p149).

## SCORING AND GLAZING HAM

**1 Using a sharp knife**, score the fat down to the meat in a criss-cross pattern. This will allow the glaze to penetrate and flavor the meat.

**2 Using a palette knife**, spread some of the glaze mixture evenly over the scored fat.

# PORK CHOPS WITH APPLE AND BACON COMPOTE

Transform a simple midweek dinner dish with a sweet, salty apple compote, made using the meaty pan juices.

★ **SERVES** 4
★ **PREP TIME** 10 mins
★ **COOK TIME** 25 mins

### Ingredients

4 x 1in (2.5cm) thick boneless pork loin chops (about 6oz /175g each), butterflied, all fat removed
2 tbsp olive oil
2 tbsp unsalted butter
salt and freshly ground black pepper

### For the compote

1 small red onion, finely chopped
2 thick-cut smoked bacon slices, finely chopped
1 dessert apple, peeled, cored, and finely chopped
1 tbsp finely chopped sage leaves
½ cup hot chicken stock
¼ cup half-and-half
1 tsp good-quality maple syrup

**1** To butterfly a pork chop, place it on a chopping board. Using a sharp knife, make a horizontal incision, about 1in (2.5cm) deep, down the length of the chop. Make sure that the top and bottom layers are of uniform thickness. Once you've cut the entire length, cut deeper into the loin, pulling back the top layer as you go, until you are about 1in (2.5cm) from the edge. Open up the flaps, as you would a book, and lay them flat on the board. Remove any fat. Repeat for the remaining chops.

**2** In a large, heavy-based frying pan, heat 1 tbsp each of the oil and butter. Season the pork chops well and pan-fry for 3–4 minutes on each side, until well browned and cooked through. If you only have room to fry 2 at a time, keep the cooked ones warm in an oven at a low temperature, loosely covered with foil, while you fry the rest, adding a little extra oil and butter, if necessary.

**3** While the pork is resting, heat the remaining oil and butter in the pan. Add the onion and cook over medium heat for 5 minutes, until softened but not browned. Add the bacon and cook for 2 minutes, or until crisp. Finally, add the apple and sage, and cook for 2 minutes, or until the apple begins to soften.

**4** Increase the heat and add the chicken stock. Allow the mixture to bubble up, then add the half-and-half and maple syrup. Reduce the heat to a low simmer and cook the compote for about 5 minutes, or until the liquid has reduced, leaving a thick, rich sauce. Adjust the seasoning, if necessary, and serve alongside the pork chops, with the mashed potatoes from p156 and the collard greens from p148.

**COOK'S TIP** When you are ready to serve the pork chops, carefully drain any cooking liquid that has gathered in the warming dish into the compote, for added flavor. If it makes the compote too thin, cook for a further 1–2 minutes to reduce the liquid.

# MAC 'N' CHEESE

A thick, creamy mac 'n' cheese is everybody's idea of a tasty supper—the ultimate family favorite.

★ **SERVES** 4
★ **PREP TIME** 10 mins
★ **COOK TIME** 15 mins

### Ingredients

2¾ cups dried macaroni
salt and freshly ground
  black pepper
3½ tbsp butter
½ cup all-purpose flour
2 cups whole milk
1⅓ cups grated sharp
  cheddar cheese
½ cup finely grated
  Parmesan cheese
steamed broccoli, to serve

**1** Cook the macaroni in boiling salted water according to the package instructions. Drain and transfer to a shallow ovenproof dish.

**2** Meanwhile, melt the butter in a saucepan. Whisk in the flour over low heat and cook for 2 minutes, whisking constantly, until the mixture begins to bubble and separate.

**3** Take the pan off the heat and whisk in the milk, a little at a time, whisking well between each addition, until it has all been added and the sauce is smooth. Return to the heat and cook, stirring until the sauce thickens. Reduce the heat to low and cook, stirring occasionally, for 5 minutes. Be sure to whisk right into the edges of the saucepan, as this is where the sauce can burn if left undisturbed. Add 1 cup of the cheddar cheese and stir until it has melted.

**4** Preheat the broiler on its highest setting. Pour the sauce over the macaroni, season with pepper, and stir well to coat. Sprinkle over the remaining cheddar cheese and the Parmesan. Place on a baking sheet and broil for 5 minutes, or until bubbling. Serve with steamed broccoli.

**Dried pasta** is a pantry essential. Try to keep a few different shapes on hand.

## NOW TRY...

## TOMATO & RICOTTA

For a lighter version, heat ¾ cup of **cream cheese** over low heat with 1 cup **ricotta** and 2 heaped tbsp of all-purpose flour. Bring to a boil, stirring until it melts. Add ⅔ cup of grated Parmesan and season well. Pour over the cooked pasta, add some chopped **basil** and 12 halved **cherry tomatoes**, and broil as usual.

## TUNA & PETIT POIS

Add 1 can **tuna**, drained and mashed, and 5½oz (150g) frozen **petit pois** to the sauce at the end of step 3 and cook as directed.

## MAC 'N' CHEESE BALLS

Turn leftover mac 'n' cheese into delicious appetizers. Roll tablespoons of the mixture between damp palms to form small balls. Coat in flour, then a little **beaten egg**, then some **Parmesan-flavored breadcrumbs**. Deep-fry in batches of 4 for 2–3 minutes in hot oil (about 350°F/180°C), turning occasionally, until golden brown and crispy.

# RED BEANS AND QUINOA

Red beans and rice is a classic Creole dish. Using quinoa instead of rice gives it a healthy, modern twist.

- ★ **SERVES** 4-6
- ★ **PREP TIME** 15 mins
- ★ **COOK TIME** 1 hr

**Ingredients**

1 tbsp olive oil
3 garlic cloves, crushed
1 onion, chopped
1 green bell pepper, seeded
  and chopped
1 red bell pepper, seeded
  and chopped
2 x 14oz (400g) can red kidney
  beans, drained
14oz (400g) can chopped
  tomatoes
1lb (450g) spicy turkey sausage
salt and black pepper
1 tsp red pepper flakes
1 tsp finely chopped thyme
1 tsp finely chopped sage
2 cups brown or red quinoa

**1** In a large saucepan, heat the oil over medium heat. Sauté the garlic, then stir in the onion and cook until browned. Add the peppers, beans, and tomatoes, then reduce the heat to a simmer.

**2** Cook the sausages in a frying pan for 10 minutes. Remove from the pan, cut into $\frac{1}{2}$in (1cm) slices, and stir into the vegetable mixture, along with the seasoning, red pepper flakes, thyme, and sage. Simmer, uncovered, for 45 minutes.

**3** Meanwhile, add the quinoa to a large, heavy-based saucepan filled with $4\frac{1}{4}$ cups of water. Bring to a boil, then reduce to a simmer, cover, and cook for 30 minutes, or until all the water has been absorbed. Fluff the quinoa with a fork and serve, topped with the sausage and vegetable mixture.

**COOK'S TIP** For a vegetarian version, simply omit the turkey sausage and cook as usual.

**Quinoa**, a newly fashionable but ancient superfood, is a great source of plant-based protein.

# VEGETABLE FAJITAS WITH CILANTRO CREAM

Prepare all the vegetables beforehand, as fajitas require cooking the ingredients fast and serving them hot.

★ **SERVES** 4
★ **PREP TIME** 15 mins
★ **COOK TIME** 15 mins

### Ingredients

4 large Portobello
   mushrooms, sliced
2 ears of corn
2 tbsp olive oil, for frying
2 garlic cloves, crushed
1 jalapeño or other mild green
   chile, finely chopped
3 medium onions,
   roughly chopped
1 large green bell pepper,
   seeded and roughly chopped
8 small tortillas

### For the marinade

1 tbsp olive oil
juice of 3 limes
1 tsp chipotle paste
salt and freshly ground
   black pepper

### For the cilantro cream

¾ cup Greek yogurt
juice of 1 lime
bunch of cilantro, chopped

**1** To make the marinade, mix together the oil, lime juice, and chipotle paste in a bowl and season to taste. Stir in the mushroom slices, cover, and marinate for 10 minutes. For the cilantro cream, mix together the yogurt, lime juice, and cilantro in a small bowl.

**2** Hold the corn upright on a board and, with a sharp knife, cut downward to shear off the kernels (see technique, p152). Heat the oil in a deep, straight-sided frying pan. Add the garlic, jalapeño, onions, pepper, and corn kernels. Cook, stirring frequently, for 3–5 minutes, or until golden brown and cooked through. Remove the vegetables from the pan.

**3** Add the mushrooms, along with the marinade, to the pan and cook over medium to high heat for 1–2 minutes on each side until brown.

**4** Layer the tortillas with the fajita vegetables, mushrooms, and cilantro cream. Serve hot.

# JALAPEÑO, ONION, AND CHEDDAR HUSHPUPPIES

These bite-sized treats are made with deep-fried cornbread batter, enhanced with spicy jalapeños and salty cheese.

★ **MAKES** 20
★ **PREP TIME** 15 mins, plus resting
★ **COOK TIME** 15 mins

**Ingredients**

1 cup yellow cornmeal
½ cup self-rising flour
1 tsp baking powder
1 tsp sugar
½ tsp cayenne pepper
½ tsp salt
freshly ground black pepper
1 cup finely grated sharp Cheddar cheese
1 large jalapeño or other mild green chile, finely chopped
4 large scallions, trimmed and finely chopped
1 cup buttermilk (or to make your own, see p12)
1 egg
1¾ pints (1 liter) peanut or sunflower oil, for frying

**1** Sift the cornmeal, flour, baking powder, sugar, cayenne pepper, and salt into a large bowl and season well with black pepper. Add the cheese, jalapeño, and scallions and mix well to combine.

**2** Whisk together the buttermilk and egg in a bowl. Make a well in the center of the dry ingredients and whisk in the buttermilk to form a thick batter. Leave to rest for 10 minutes.

**3** In a large, heavy-based saucepan or deep-fat fryer, heat the oil to 375°F (190°C), as shown in the technique on p144. Using a lightly greased tablespoon measurer, form small, rounded spoonfuls of the batter and drop them quickly into the hot oil.

**4** Cook for 2–3 minutes, turning occasionally, until they are puffed up and golden brown all over. Remove the cooked hushpuppies from the oil with a metal slotted spoon and drain them on paper towels. Serve immediately.

**COOK'S TIP** When deep-frying, do not overcrowd the pan as the hushpuppies will not brown well. It is better to cook in batches. Never fill a pan more than half full with oil, as its level will rise when you add the hushpuppies, and could cause the hot oil to bubble over.

# ONION RINGS WITH CHIPOTLE AÏOLI

This tasty side dish is an excellent accompaniment to dry-rub steak (see p128) and also works as a stand-alone appetizer.

★ **MAKES** 20
★ **PREP TIME** 15 mins
★ **COOK TIME** 15 mins

### Ingredients

1¾ pints (1 liter) peanut or
   sunflower oil, for frying
1 cup all-purpose flour
1 tsp ground chipotle or smoked
   paprika
½ tsp cayenne pepper
½ tsp salt
1 large onion
1 cup milk
2 eggs
2 cups fresh white breadcrumbs
1 tbsp hot sauce

### For the aïoli

1 cup mayonnaise
1 tbsp ground chipotle or
   smoked paprika
4 garlic cloves, diced
juice of 1 lemon

**1** In a large, heavy-based saucepan or deep-fat fryer, heat the oil to 375°F (190°C) for deep-frying (see technique, below). In a medium bowl, combine the flour, paprika, cayenne pepper, and salt.

**2** Peel and cut the onion into ½in (1cm) slices and pull apart the rings. Toss the onion rings in the flour mixture, remove and set aside.

**3** Add the milk, eggs, breadcrumbs, and hot sauce to the flour mixture. Dip the onion rings in the batter, coating evenly on both sides, and fry them in the oil for 3–4 minutes, or until golden brown. Remove with a slotted spoon and let them cool slightly on a wire rack.

**4** While the rings are frying, mix together all the ingredients for the aïoli in a small bowl. Serve the onion rings hot with the aïoli.

## HEATING OIL FOR DEEP-FRYING

**1 Add the oil** to the saucepan or deep-fat fryer, filling it no more than half full. Heat to 375°F (190°C) and add a cube of bread to test if the oil is ready.

**2 Leave the bread** to sizzle in the oil for 1 minute. If the oil is hot enough, the bread should turn golden brown. Remove with a slotted spoon.

# WARM EDAMAME SUCCOTASH

Although lima beans are more traditionally used in succotash, edamame give this salad a pleasing bite and modern twist.

★ **SERVES** 4
★ **PREP TIME** 10 mins
★ **COOK TIME** 10-12 mins

### Ingredients

2 corn cobs
1½ cups frozen, shelled edamame (soy beans)
2 tbsp olive oil
1 small red onion, finely chopped
2 garlic cloves, finely chopped
½ cup bacon, finely diced
2 tbsp balsamic vinegar
1 tsp soy sauce
½ tsp sugar
salt and freshly ground black pepper
¾ cup cherry tomatoes, halved
2 scallions, trimmed and finely chopped
2 heaped tbsp mint, finely chopped, plus extra to serve

**1** Hold the corn cob upright on a chopping board and, using a sharp knife, cut down the sides to release the kernels (see technique, p152). Put the kernels and edamame in a large pan of boiling water and cook for 2–3 minutes until just cooked, but still al dente. Drain the vegetables and put them in a bowl of ice water—this will help to stop the cooking process and preserve their color. Drain well and set aside.

**2** Heat the oil in a large, heavy-based frying pan over medium heat. Cook the onion for 5 minutes, until softened but not browned. Add the garlic and bacon, and cook for a further 3–4 minutes until the bacon is crispy.

**3** Remove from the heat and stir in the vinegar, soy sauce, and sugar, and season well. Add the corn and edamame mix, tomatoes, scallions, and mint to the pan and stir well to combine. Pour the salad out into a serving bowl and scatter with more mint, if desired. Serve warm or at room temperature.

**COOK'S TIP** If edamame are not available, try using small fava beans instead. For best results, briefly blanch the beans and peel to reveal their bright green flesh.

**Cherry tomatoes** are sweet, sharp, and acidic, and add color and flavor to any dish.

# BOSTON BAKED BEANS

These beans are cooked to a traditional recipe that dates back to the time of the first settlers to America.

- ★ **SERVES** 4-6
- ★ **PREP TIME** 15 mins
- ★ **COOK TIME** 2½ hrs

### Ingredients

10oz (300g) thick-cut
  smoked bacon, chopped,
  or diced pancetta
3 x 14oz (400g) can Great
  Northern beans or
  cannellini beans
10oz (300g) onion, diced
3 garlic cloves, chopped
1½ cups molasses
1 tsp garlic powder
¼ cup apple cider vinegar
2 tsp mustard powder
1 tsp paprika
2 tsp salt and pinch
  of freshly ground
  black pepper
⅓ cup chopped parsley,
  to garnish

**1** Preheat the oven to 325°F (160°C). In a heavy-based soup pot or flameproof casserole, brown the bacon over high heat for 5 minutes on each side. Remove from the pot and set aside.

**2** Add 1 can of beans with their juices and one-third of the onion to the pot, then add one-third of the garlic over it and top with one-third of the bacon. Repeat to make two more layers.

**3** In a medium bowl, whisk together the molasses, garlic powder, vinegar, mustard powder, paprika, and salt and pepper. Pour over the bean mixture, then bake, uncovered, in the oven for 2½ hours. Season to taste, and serve hot, garnished with the parsley.

**Molasses** has a rich, dark, toffee-like flavor.

## NOW TRY...

### TEX-MEX TWIST

Substitute the Great Northern beans with the same quantity of **black beans**, and replace the molasses with a 14oz can **chopped tomatoes** (with their juices) and 1 tbsp **chipotle paste**.

### VEGAN OPTION

Replace the bacon with 1¼ cup **slivered almonds** and substitute 1 can of Great Northern beans with 1 can of **chickpeas**.

### HONEY & KETCHUP

Try a brown sugar variation by substituting the molasses with the same amount of **honey** and adding ¼ cup **brown sugar** and ½ cup **ketchup**.

# COLLARD GREENS AGRODOLCE

Agrodolce, a traditional Italian sweet-and-sour sauce, is given an American twist here with the use of maple syrup.

★ **SERVES** 4
★ **PREP TIME** 15 mins
★ **COOK TIME** 15–20 mins

**Ingredients**

3 tbsp olive oil
1 large onion, finely diced
4½oz (125g) pancetta,
    finely chopped
2 garlic cloves, crushed
10oz (300g) collard greens
    or spring greens, de-ribbed
    and finely shredded,
    prepared weight
¾ cup hot chicken stock
salt and freshly ground
    black pepper
2 tbsp balsamic vinegar
1 tbsp maple syrup

**1** Heat the oil in a large, heavy-based saucepan over medium heat. Fry the onion over medium heat for 5 minutes, until softened but not browned. Add the pancetta and cook for 2 minutes, until it begins to crisp up. Then add the garlic and cook for a further minute.

**2** Add the shredded greens to the pan, in 2 batches if necessary, to allow them to wilt. Toss them in the onion and pancetta. Add the stock and season well. Bring the pan to a boil, reduce to a simmer, and cook, covered, for 5 minutes, until the greens have wilted.

**3** Remove the lid and increase the heat to high. Cook the greens for a further 5 minutes, stirring frequently, until the liquid has evaporated and the greens are soft.

**4** Add the vinegar and maple syrup, and cook for a minute until the remaining liquid has reduced to a syrupy glaze. Check the seasoning and serve.

**Collard greens** are a favorite green of the South, but any dark leafy greens can be used as substitutes.

# GREEN BEAN CASSEROLE

This modern twist on a classic Thanksgiving side has the green beans smothered in a rich, garlicky sauce before baking.

★ **SERVES** 6-8
★ **PREP TIME** 15 mins
★ **COOK TIME** 40 mins

### Ingredients

2 cups heavy cream
2 tbsp all-purpose flour
8 tbsps (1 stick) butter, diced
3 garlic cloves, crushed
salt and freshly ground
   black pepper
8oz (225g) button mushrooms,
   quartered
1lb (450g) green beans, trimmed
1 tbsp olive oil
3½oz (100g) shallots, sliced
   into thin rings

**1** Preheat the oven to 350°F (180°C). In a saucepan, whisk together the cream, flour, butter, garlic, and seasoning over medium heat. Simmer for 5 minutes, or until thickened. Stir in the mushrooms and simmer for a further 15 minutes.

**2** Meanwhile, bring a large saucepan of salted water to a boil and blanch the beans for 45–60 seconds, or until they turn bright green. Drain, and rinse them in cold water to stop the cooking process.

**3** In a frying pan, heat the oil and quickly sauté the shallots over medium-high heat until they brown. Spread the beans evenly in a flameproof casserole and pour over the mushroom cream sauce. Sprinkle the shallots over the sauce and bake, uncovered, for 30–35 minutes, or until the beans are tender but still retain some bite. Serve hot with Garlic buttered roasted turkey (see p94).

# COLESLAW

Light on the mayo and with a mild heat of mustard and chile, this coleslaw makes a perfect side dish.

★ **SERVES** 6

★ **PREP TIME** 20 mins

### Ingredients

½ cup mayonnaise
¼ cup apple cider vinegar
1 tsp mustard powder
1 tbsp brown mustard
1 tsp garlic powder
1 tsp red pepper flakes
salt and freshly ground
    black pepper
½ green cabbage
1 red onion, thinly sliced
4 small carrots, grated
3 celery stalks,
    thinly sliced

**1** In a medium bowl, mix together the mayonnaise, vinegar, powdered and brown mustards, garlic powder, and red pepper flakes. Season well.

**2** Hold the cabbage, cut-side down, on a chopping board and cut in half lengthwise, straight through the stalk. Slice out the core from each wedge and cut across the cabbage, creating broad or fine shreds. Transfer to a large bowl.

**3** Add the other vegetables and mix well until the vegetables are well coated in the mayonnaise. Served chilled.

## SERVE WITH

### DELI-STYLE
# REUBEN
SEE PAGE 80

### SOUTHERN FRIED
# CHICKEN
SEE PAGE 96

## NOW TRY...

### ASIAN SLAW
Combine 1 shredded **cabbage**, 2 grated **carrots**, 1 sliced **red pepper**, a handful of chopped **cilantro**, 4 tbsp **rice vinegar**, 2 tbsp **sesame oil**, 2 tbsp **sesame sauce**, 1 tbsp crushed **ginger**, and 1 tbsp crushed **garlic**. Season to taste.

### BROCCOLI & BACON
Toss 1 chopped **raw broccoli head** with 1 cup crumbled smoked **bacon**, ½ cup **mayonnaise**, 1 tbsp **Dijon mustard**, and ¼ cup **apple cider vinegar**. Season to taste.

### APPLE & CARROT
Grate 3 **red apples** and 3 **carrots**, and toss with ¼ cup **apple cider vinegar**, ½ cup **mayonnaise**, and ¾ cup **dried cherries**. Season well.

# CREAMED CORN WITH BASIL AND PARMESAN

Here, fresh corn is cooked in the style of a risotto, with Parmesan and basil added to complete the Italian feel.

★ **SERVES** 4-6

★ **PREP TIME** 10 mins

★ **COOK TIME** 30 mins

**Ingredients**

4 corn cobs, about 1lb 2oz
(500g), kernel weight

4 tbsp unsalted butter

2 tsp olive oil

1 onion, finely chopped

1 cup good-quality hot chicken
or vegetable stock

½ cup heavy cream

1 tsp all-purpose flour

½ cup finely grated Parmesan
cheese

2 tbsp finely chopped basil

salt and freshly ground
black pepper

**1** Remove the kernels and "milk" from the corn cobs, as shown in the technique below. Try using really young, fresh corn for this recipe, as the skins will be softer and easier to break down on cooking.

**2** Melt the butter and oil in a medium, heavy-based saucepan. Add the onion and cook over low heat for 5 minutes, until softened but not browned. Add the corn and its juices along with the stock to the pan; the corn should be barely covered by the liquid. Bring to a boil, reduce to a simmer, and cook, covered, for 15 minutes, until the corn starts to soften. If you prefer a smoother, creamed corn, use a hand-held blender to partially liquidize the corn while it is still in the pan.

**3** Remove the lid, add the cream, sprinkle over the flour, and increase the heat. Cook over high heat, stirring frequently, for 7–10 minutes, until the cream has reduced and thickened and the corn is soft. Remove from the heat, then stir in the Parmesan and basil. Season to taste at the end of the cooking time. Salting at the beginning may cause the skin of the kernels to toughen and result in a less creamy texture.

## REMOVING CORN KERNELS

1 **Hold the corn cob upright** on a chopping board and use a sharp knife to cut down the sides to release the kernels. Rotate the cob and repeat.

2 **To extract the "milk,"** hold the cob upright in a bowl and scrape down the sides with the knife's blunt edge. This starchy juice will thicken the dish.

# GRILLED CORN WITH LIME AND CHILI BUTTER

This butter is an easy way to flavor grilled vegetables, meat, or fish. It freezes well for up to 6 months.

★ **SERVES** 4
★ **PREP TIME** 10 mins
★ **COOK TIME** 10 mins, plus freezing

**Ingredients**

7 tbsp unsalted butter, softened
finely grated zest of 1 lime
½ tsp chili powder or
  cayenne pepper
½ tsp salt
freshly ground black pepper
4 corn cobs
a little olive oil

**1** Prepare a grill for cooking. In a small bowl, mash the butter with the lime zest, chili powder, and salt and pepper.

**2** Cut a piece of parchment paper, about 6in (15cm) square. Put the butter in the middle of one edge of the paper and shape it like a sausage. Roll the butter sausage up in the paper, then twist the ends so the butter forms a tight shape. Leave in the freezer for at least 30 minutes before use (or freeze until needed).

**3** Cook the corn cobs in a large pan of boiling water for up to 5 minutes until the corn is tender (this will depend on the size and age of the cobs). Drain well, rub them in a little oil, and grill for 6 minutes over hot coals or flame, turning them frequently, until they are lightly charred on all sides.

**4** Serve the corn with a ½in- (1cm-) thick disk of the chilled butter on top to melt.

# A taste of the
# MIDWEST

## FOODS AND FLAVORS

★ **Pierogi**, a type of stuffed dumpling, was popularized by Polish immigrants to the region.

★ **Chili** is known as a classic from the Southwest, but the Midwest has its own version, too, which is mildly spiced with cinnamon and cloves.

★ Scandinavian immigrants introduced **lefse**—thin tortilla-like pancakes made from flour and mashed potatoes.

★ As well as the **wheat**, **corn**, and **potatoes** grown on the Great Plains, the rich grasslands are a center for **beef** production.

★ **Iowa** is an important center of pork production for the US.

★ Chicago is home to **"deep-dish" pizza**, which is famously thick—and heavy with sauce and cheese.

*Pot-roasting is an easy way to get the maximum flavor and tenderness out of cheaper cuts of meat.*

The landlocked states of the Midwest, known as both the "heartland" and "breadbasket" of America, are home to vast plains of wheat, corn, and soybeans.

The German immigrants that first settled here in the 1700s were soon followed by settlers from Britain, and Northern and Eastern Europe—notably Scandinavia and Poland. The food they brought with them was homespun, comforting, and ideal for the long, cold winters of the region.

When people gathered to eat as families or in large community groups, stews, casseroles, and one-pot dishes were the main staples. Usually full of meat, potatoes, and vegetables, they were easy to prepare, satisfying, nutritious, and a great way to feed large numbers of people.

The settlers soon found that the rivers of the Midwest were teeming with freshwater trout—making up for a lack of seafood. The land to the north thronged with elk and venison, and, during the summer, fresh huckleberries—a wild crop similar to blueberries that still resists cultivation—abounded.

*The fertile flatlands of the Great Plains are home to huge arable farms.*

**The pasty, a hand pie stuffed with meat, potatoes, and turnips, arrived with the Cornish tin miners, who came to the area around Michigan in the mid-19th century to work in the mines of the Upper Peninsula.**

A sloppy joe sandwich is full of flavor, but something of a challenge to eat without making a mess!

Potato salad can be made in many ways, but a classic mayonnaise-based one is always popular.

Chicago—the home of deep-dish pizza, hotdogs, and Italian beef sandwiches.

Mac 'n' cheese may be the ultimate comfort food, and everyone has their own spin on this classic dish.

# GARLIC AND SHALLOT MASHED POTATOES

For an indulgent treat, nothing beats these creamy mashed potatoes with caramelized shallots and garlic.

★ **SERVES** 4
★ **PREP TIME** 15 mins
★ **COOK TIME** 25 mins

**Ingredients**

5 large potatoes, such as Russet, cut into quarters
8 tbsps butter, diced, plus extra for frying
2 shallots, sliced into rings
2 garlic cloves, crushed
½ cup sour cream
juice of 1 lemon
salt and freshly ground black pepper

**1** Leaving the skins on, cook the potatoes in a saucepan of boiling water for about 20 minutes, or until tender.

**2** Meanwhile, in a frying pan, heat a pat of butter over medium heat and sauté the shallots and garlic until softened and browned.

**3** When the potatoes have softened, drain well and transfer them to a large bowl. With the skin still on, use a potato masher or fork to mash the potatoes.

**4** Stir in the sour cream, butter, lemon juice, and the sautéed shallots and garlic. Season to taste and serve hot.

## PEELING GARLIC

**1 Place each garlic clove** on a chopping board. Cover with the flat side of a large knife and pound with the palm of your hand.

**2 Peel away the papery skin** and discard it. Then cut off the ends of each clove, and finely chop or crush the garlic.

# SWEET POTATO PARMESAN TOTS

Sweet, salty, and slightly spicy, these bite-sized treats make a great accompaniment to any meal.

★ **MAKES** 30
★ **PREP TIME** 20 mins
★ **COOK TIME** 40 mins, plus cooling

## Ingredients

4 large sweet potatoes
⅔ cup grated Parmesan cheese
¼ cup all-purpose flour
1 tsp garlic powder
1 tsp mustard seeds
1 tsp cayenne pepper
1¾ pints (1 liter) peanut or sunflower oil, for frying

**For the honey mustard dip**
¼ cup Dijon mustard
¼ cup mayonnaise
¼ cup honey

**1** Boil the sweet potatoes for 10–15 minutes, or until cooked but firm. The potatoes should be soft enough to be easily pierced with a fork, but firm enough to be grated.

**2** Allow the potatoes to cool until you can comfortably handle them. Once cool enough, peel off the skin and grate the potatoes. Combine the grated potatoes with the Parmesan cheese, flour, garlic powder, mustard seeds, and cayenne pepper.

**3** In a large, heavy-based saucepan or deep-fat fryer, heat the oil to 375°F (190°C), as shown in the technique on p144. Take about 1 tbsp of the potato mixture and roll it between your palms to form a ball. Repeat to make the remaining balls.

**4** Fry the balls in batches of 6 for 2–3 minutes each, or until brown. Remove them with a slotted spoon and let them rest on a wire rack while you fry the remaining balls.

**5** For the honey mustard dip, combine the mustard, mayonnaise, and honey in a small bowl. Stir well to incorporate all the ingredients. Serve the tots hot with the dip.

**Sweet potatoes** are a healthy, vitamin-packed alternative to white potatoes.

# RAINBOW POTATO GRATIN

Try layering as many different-colored potatoes
as you can find for this eye-catching dish.

★ **SERVES** 4
★ **PREP TIME** 20 mins
★ **COOK TIME** 45 mins

### Ingredients

2lb (900g) sweet potatoes;
   purple potatoes, such as
   salad blue; and yellow, waxy
   potatoes (total weight)
2 cups heavy cream
4 garlic cloves, crushed
2 cups grated Cheddar cheese
salt and freshly ground
   black pepper
pinch of red pepper flakes

**1** Preheat the oven to 350°F (180°C). Leaving the skin on, scrub the potatoes well and cut them into thin slices (see the technique below). In a small saucepan, add the cream and garlic, and bring to a boil over medium heat. Remove from the heat and set aside.

**2** In a medium flameproof casserole, layer the potatoes and cheese, sprinkling a little salt and pepper between each layer. Finish with a generous layer of cheese.

**3** Pour the cream around the edge of the potatoes, so as not to disturb the layers. Season well and add a pinch of red pepper flakes. Bake for 45 minutes, or until the potatoes are golden brown and the cheese starts to bubble.

**COOK'S TIP** If salad blue potatoes are not available, try using fresh beets instead.

## SLICING A POTATO

**To cut with a knife,** hold the potato firmly on a chopping board and cut it into slices of uniform thickness, as desired.

**If using a mandolin,** hold the potato in the carrier to protect your fingers as you slide it up and down the sharp blade, which can be adjusted.

# SLOW-COOKED BLACK BEANS

It's a good idea to make more than you'll need, as these versatile beans keep well and the flavour improves overnight.

- ★ **SERVES** 4–6
- ★ **PREP TIME** 20 mins, plus soaking
- ★ **COOK TIME** 1½ hrs

**Ingredients**

1 cup dried black beans
2 tbsp olive oil
1 red onion, finely chopped
1 large garlic clove, finely chopped
1 large jalapeño or other mild green chilli, finely chopped
⅓ cup pancetta, finely diced
3 cups hot chicken stock
freshly ground black pepper
chopped cilantro leaves, to garnish (optional)
sour cream, to serve (optional)

**1** Put the dried beans in a large bowl, cover well with cold water, and allow them to soak overnight. The beans will swell as they soak, so leave enough room for them to expand. Drain the beans and rinse them well under cold running water.

**2** Heat the oil in a medium, heavy-based saucepan. Fry the onion over a medium heat for 5 minutes, until softened but not browned. Add the garlic and jalapeño and cook for another minute. Finally, add the pancetta and cook for 3–4 minutes, until crispy and golden brown.

**3** Add the beans and chicken stock to the pan. Season to taste with pepper (the stock and pancetta are salty). Bring to the boil, reduce to a low simmer, and cook, uncovered, for 1 hour, or until the cooking liquid is reduced.

**4** Cover and cook on a very low heat for 30–45 minutes, until the beans are tender and the liquid has reduced and thickened. Serve on its own, or with a sprinkling of cilantro and a bowl of sour cream on the side.

**Dried black beans**, a mainstay of Mexican cuisine, have a rich smoky flavour.

# CORNMEAL-CRUSTED FRIED OKRA

Cornmeal (you can also use fine polenta) gives a crunchy coating to deep-fried food. Use young okra for the best result.

★ **SERVES** 6–8
★ **PREP TIME** 15 mins
★ **COOK TIME** 15–20 mins

**Ingredients**

1 cup all-purpose flour
2 tsp smoked paprika or ancho chile powder
1 tsp cayenne pepper
2 tsp salt
2 large eggs
1 cup cornmeal or fine polenta
24 okra, cut into ½in (1cm) slices
1¾ pints (1 liter) peanut or sunflower oil, for frying
apple cider vinegar, to serve

**1** In a bowl, combine the flour with 1 tsp smoked paprika, ½ tsp cayenne pepper, and 1 tsp salt, and set aside. Whisk the eggs in a second bowl. In a third bowl, mix the cornmeal with the remaining smoked paprika, cayenne pepper, and salt.

**2** Toss the okra in the flour mixture, dip each briefly in the eggs, then coat well in the cornmeal mixture.

**3** Heat the oil to 375°F (190°C) in a large, heavy-based saucepan or deep-fat fryer, as shown in the technique on p144. Fry the okra, in batches, in the hot oil for 3–5 minutes, or until golden brown.

**4** Remove them with a slotted spoon and let them cool on a wire rack while you fry the remaining batches. Serve with apple cider vinegar as a dip for a tangy twist.

# SWEET POTATO CASSEROLE WITH BACON

Traditionally served with turkey at Thanksgiving, the smooth, sweet potato contrasts well with the crunchy, salty topping.

★ **SERVES** 8

★ **PREP TIME** 20 mins

★ **COOK TIME** 1 hr

### Ingredients

4lb (1.8kg) sweet potatoes, peeled and chopped

4 eggs

1¾ cups sugar

3 sticks (1½ cups) unsalted butter, melted and cooled

1 cup milk

1 tsp vanilla extract

### For the topping

1lb (450g) thick-cut smoked bacon

1 tbsp ground cinnamon

2 tbsp sugar

4 tbsp butter

1 cup light brown sugar

1 cup chopped pecans

**1** Preheat the oven to 350°F (180°C). Cook the potatoes in a saucepan of boiling water for 10–15 minutes, or until tender. Drain well, mash until smooth, and set aside.

**2** In a frying pan, dry-fry the bacon over medium-high heat for 10–15 minutes, turning occasionally, until evenly browned and crisp. Remove from the pan and drain on paper towels. Sprinkle with the cinnamon and sugar. Set aside. When it is cool enough to handle, crumble the bacon.

**3** Place the eggs, sugar, and melted butter in a large bowl and, using a balloon whisk or an electric hand whisk, whisk until well combined; the mixture should be golden and silky. Add the milk and vanilla extract, then mix in the potatoes until well blended. Spoon the mixture into a large ovenproof casserole with a capacity of about 7 pints (4 liters).

**4** Melt the butter and combine with the brown sugar, crumbled bacon pieces, and pecans. Sprinkle over the potato mixture in the casserole. Bake in the oven for 45 minutes. If the topping starts to brown, cover the dish with foil. Serve hot.

**COOK'S TIP** For a much-loved take on this festive casserole, mix 1½oz (45g) mini marshmallows into the topping mixture.

**Pecans**, a Southern crop, are used there in both savory and sweet dishes.

# FRIED GREEN TOMATOES WITH BASIL CREAM

A crispy coating and herbed cream dip turn these firm tomatoes into an irresistibly tasty side dish.

★ **SERVES** 4

★ **PREP TIME** 15–20 mins, plus soaking and resting

★ **COOK TIME** 15 mins

### Ingredients

8 green tomatoes

¾ cup buttermilk (or to make your own, see p12)

½ tsp smoked paprika or ancho chile powder

salt and freshly ground black pepper

⅓ cup cornmeal or fine polenta

⅓ cup panko or day-old breadcrumbs

¼ cup finely grated Parmesan cheese

3 tbsp finely chopped basil

4 cups peanut or sunflower oil, for frying

¾ cup crème fraîche or sour cream

finely grated zest of ½ lemon

**1** Slice the tops and bottoms off the tomatoes and, depending on the size of the tomatoes, cut them into 2 or 3 equal slices, about ¼in (5mm) thick. Lay them in a single layer in a large, shallow dish. Whisk the buttermilk with the smoked paprika and season well. Pour the buttermilk over the tomatoes. Cover with plastic wrap and chill for at least 2 hours before cooking.

**2** Place the cornmeal, breadcrumbs, and Parmesan in a food processor and pulse until well combined. Mix in 1 tbsp of the chopped basil and season well.

**3** When the tomatoes have soaked, drain them well. Toss them in the cornmeal crust, making sure that they are evenly coated on all sides, then leave them to rest for at least 30 minutes on a wire rack to allow the coating to set a little—this will help it to stick during frying.

**4** Pour the oil into a large, heavy-based frying pan to a depth of at least ½in (1cm). When the oil is hot, add the tomatoes, being careful not to overcrowd the pan. Cook them for 2–3 minutes, turning them once, until they are golden brown on both sides. Remove them with a slotted spoon and let them rest on a wire rack.

**5** To make the basil cream, whisk together the crème fraîche, the remaining basil and lemon zest, and season well.

**Green tomatoes** are simply underripe red tomatoes, and have a fresh, delicate taste.

# SPICED CRANBERRY AND ORANGE SAUCE

Fresh cranberries need some sugar to counter their acidity. This sauce is perfect served with roasted turkey (see p94).

★ **SERVES** 8
★ **PREP TIME** 5 mins
★ **COOK TIME** 10 mins

**Ingredients**
3 heaped cups cranberries
1 cup fresh orange juice
finely grated zest of 1 large
   orange (see technique, below)
1 cinnamon stick
½ cup sugar
⅓ cup light brown sugar
1 tbsp maple syrup

**1** Put the cranberries in a small, heavy-based saucepan and cover them with the orange juice. Add the orange zest, cinnamon stick, and sugars.

**2** Bring the liquid to a boil, then reduce to a simmer and cook over low heat for 10 minutes, stirring occasionally, until the cranberries have softened and burst, and the mixture has thickened and reduced.

**3** Take the sauce off the heat, remove the cinnamon stick, and stir in the maple syrup. Serve the sauce either warm or at room temperature. You can also use it cold in a leftover turkey sandwich, mixed with good-quality mayonnaise or in the Grilled cheese sandwich from p90.

## ZESTING AN ORANGE

**For grated zest**, hold the orange firmly in one hand and rub it diagonally, rather than vertically, across the fine holes of a grater.

**For threadlike strips**, hold the orange firmly in one hand and scrape its surface with a zester to create threadlike strips.

# REFRIED BLACK BEANS WITH PICO DE GALLO

Enjoy this Mexican-style side dish of mashed beans with a tomato salsa over rice for a satisfying meat-free meal.

★ **SERVES** 6
★ **PREP TIME** 15 mins
★ **COOK TIME** 2 hrs

**Ingredients**

1lb (450g) dried black beans
1 onion, roughly chopped
3 garlic cloves, roughly chopped
salt and freshly ground
    black pepper
1 tsp olive oil

**For the pico de gallo**

2 tomatoes, diced
1 red onion, finely chopped
handful of cilantro
    leaves, chopped
juice of 2 limes

**To serve**

1 avocado, halved, pitted,
    and thinly sliced (see
    technique, p11)
⅓ cup grated Cheddar cheese
    (optional)
sour cream (optional)

**1** Put the dried beans, onion, and garlic into a medium soup pot. Cover with water, season, and bring to a boil over high heat. Reduce the heat and simmer, covered, for 2 hours, or until the beans turn soft. Drain the beans but reserve 1 cup of the liquid.

**2** Put the bean mixture and reserved liquid in a food processor, or use a hand-held blender, and blend until smooth.

**3** In a heavy-based saucepan, heat the oil over medium heat. Spoon the blended beans into the pan and cook, stirring frequently, for 5–6 minutes, or until thickened.

**4** To make the pico de gallo, mix the tomatoes and onion with the cilantro and lime juice. Serve the beans hot, topped with the pico de gallo, sliced avocado, and, if desired, cheese or sour cream.

## SERVE WITH

**PULLED CHICKEN TACOS**
SEE PAGE 86

**MOLE PORK ENCHILADAS**
SEE PAGE 132

# SAUSAGE AND CHESTNUT STUFFING

Fresh rosemary and chunky chestnuts add flavor and texture to this hearty bread and sausage stuffing.

★ **SERVES** 6
★ **PREP TIME** 15 mins
★ **COOK TIME** 45-50 mins

**Ingredients**
7oz (200g) spicy pork sausages
vegetable oil, for cooking
2 garlic cloves, crushed
3 shallots, sliced
1lb (450g) chestnuts, peeled
    and halved
1 loaf day-old French or
    crusty bread
1 tbsp chopped rosemary
3 cups hot chicken stock
salt and freshly ground
    black pepper

**1** Preheat the oven to 350°F (180°C). Remove the skin from the sausages and crumble the sausage meat. Heat a little oil in a frying pan and cook the sausage meat over medium heat for 5 minutes, or until browned. Remove from the pan and set aside, then fry the garlic and shallots for 5 minutes.

**2** If using raw chestnuts, rather than precooked and peeled, carve an x-shaped mark on each chestnut and boil for 10–15 minutes, or until soft. When cool enough to handle, peel back the shells to reveal the meat.

**3** Cut the bread into ½in (1cm) slices, then tear them into quarters. Put the sausages and bread into a large flameproof casserole dish. Mix in the garlic, shallots, chestnuts, and rosemary. Pour the stock over the bread mixture and season to taste.

**4** Bake for 35–40 minutes, or until crisp and browned. Serve hot with the Garlic buttered roast turkey from p94.

**Chestnuts**, with their sweet, meaty flesh, pair perfectly with sausage meat and all types of pork.

# FESTIVE CORNBREAD STUFFING

Clementines and cranberries give a seasonal flair to this colorful stuffing, traditionally served with roasted turkey.

★ **SERVES** 6-8
★ **PREP TIME** 15 mins
★ **COOK TIME** 35-40 mins

### Ingredients
4 cups crumbled cornbread (see p228)
3 garlic cloves, crushed
1 onion, finely chopped
3 clementines, peeled and segmented (see technique, below)
3oz (85g) dried cranberries
1 stick (8 tbsps) butter, diced
4 cups vegetable stock

**1** Preheat the oven to 350°F (180°C). Put the cornbread into a large mixing bowl. Add the garlic and onion, then stir in the clementines, cranberries, and butter.

**2** Add the stock and stir, making sure that the stuffing is fully incorporated. Scoop the stuffing generously into a lightly greased 9 x 9in (23 x 23cm) baking tray.

**3** Bake in the preheated oven for 35–40 minutes, or until golden brown. Remove from the oven and leave to cool for 5 minutes before placing onto a wire rack. Serve hot.

## SEGMENTING CITRUS FRUIT

**1 With a sharp knife**, slice away the top and bottom of the fruit, then work all the way around it, slicing away the skin and pith.

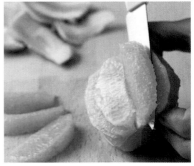

**2 Slice between each segment**, leaving the thin layer of membrane behind until you have cut out all the segments.

# DESSERTS

# PECAN AND ORANGE BANANAS FOSTER

This decadent dessert, with its rich, buttery sauce drizzled on toasted brioche, takes only minutes to prepare.

★ **SERVES** 4
★ **PREP TIME** 15 mins
★ **COOK TIME** 10 mins

**Ingredients**

½ cup pecans,
   roughly chopped
4 tbsp unsalted butter
4 heaped tbsp dark
   brown sugar
grated zest and juice of
   1 orange (see technique,
   p165)
2 large underripe (not green)
   bananas, peeled and cut
   into ½in (1cm) cubes
4 tbsp dark rum
4 thickly cut slices of brioche
   bread
4 large scoops of good-quality
   vanilla ice cream (see p194)

**1** In a large, heavy-based frying pan, dry-fry the pecans over medium heat for 3–4 minutes, stirring occasionally, until they begin to brown in places. Remove from the heat and set aside. Wipe the pan clean.

**2** Heat the butter, sugar, and the orange juice and zest (reserving a little zest for garnishing) over medium heat, stirring until the sugar dissolves. Increase the heat and cook for 2–3 minutes, until the sauce reduces slightly and begins to look glossy.

**3** Add the bananas to the pan and cook for a further 2–3 minutes over high heat, until the sauce reduces further. Meanwhile, toast the brioche. If desired, cut the bread into 2¾in (7cm) rounds.

**4** When the bananas are just tender, add the pecans and the rum and cook for 1 minute to heat it up, then use a match to carefully light the alcohol. The pan will flare up, so be careful, but the flames should die away within 1 minute.

**5** Top each brioche round with a scoop of ice cream, pour over a quarter of the caramelized bananas, and garnish with the reserved orange zest. Serve immediately.

### WHAT'S THE STORY?

Bananas Foster—a dessert flambéed with rum and served with ice cream and caramel sauce—was first made at Brennan's restaurant in New Orleans in 1951. At the time, the city was the main port of entry for imported bananas, and the dish was created in honor of regular diner and good friend of the restaurant's owner, Richard Foster.

# CHOCOLATE BREAD PUDDING

### A few pantry essentials can turn stale bread into this simple yet delicious dessert.

- ★ **SERVES** 8
- ★ **PREP TIME** 15 mins
- ★ **COOK TIME** 35 mins, plus soaking

### Ingredients

1 day-old baguette
2 cups semisweet or dark chocolate chips
4 eggs
1 tsp vanilla extract
2 cups whole milk
½ cup light brown sugar
vanilla ice cream or whipped cream, to serve

**1** Preheat the oven to 350°F (180°C). Remove the ends of the baguette and cut the bread into ½in (1cm) thick slices. Put one layer of bread in a flameproof casserole and sprinkle over some chocolate chips. Add more layers of bread, sprinkling chocolate chips between the layers as you go. Top with the remaining chips.

**2** In a bowl, mix the eggs, vanilla extract, milk, and sugar. Pour the mixture over the bread and leave to soak for 10–15 minutes.

**3** Put the casserole in the oven and bake for about 35 minutes, or until the liquid is absorbed and the bread is crisp. Slice and serve with vanilla ice cream or whipped cream.

**Baguette**, when fresh, is delicious just as it is, but leave it for a day before using in this dish.

# POUND CAKE BANANA PUDDING

This Southern version of an English trifle often uses vanilla wafers. Here, homemade pound cake makes a far tastier version.

★ **SERVES** 8–10

★ **PREP TIME** 30 mins

★ **COOK TIME** 10 mins, plus chilling

**Ingredients**

1 pound cake (see p219)
6 ripe bananas, cut into
¼in (5mm) slices

**For the pudding**

2 cups whole milk
4 tbsp cornstarch
½ cup sugar
1 tbsp butter
1 tsp vanilla extract

**For the whipped cream**

2 cups heavy cream
2 tbsp sugar
1 tsp vanilla extract

**1** Preheat the oven to 375°F (190°C). First, make the pudding. In a saucepan, bring the milk almost to a boil over high heat, then reduce the heat to a simmer. Stir in the cornstarch and sugar, and whisk continuously until thickened. Remove from the heat and add the butter and vanilla. Chill.

**2** Cut the pound cake into ½in (1cm) thick slices and toast them on a baking sheet in the oven for 10 minutes, or until both sides are well toasted. Place half the cake slices in a single layer at the bottom of a 9 x 13in (23 x 33cm) cake pan. Top with half the banana slices.

**3** Pour the pudding over the first layer evenly. Add the second layer of cake and top with the remaining bananas.

**4** In a large bowl, whisk the cream, sugar, and vanilla extract with an electric hand whisk until stiff. Using a spatula, spread it over the bananas. Chill for 45 minutes to 1 hour before serving.

# STRAWBERRY SHORTCAKE

This classic summer dessert is best served with freshly baked shortcake and ripe, juicy strawberries.

★ **MAKES** 12
★ **PREP TIME** 20 mins
★ **COOK TIME** 35 mins

### Ingredients

1½ cups all-purpose flour
½ cup cornmeal or polenta
1 tbsp baking powder
¼ tsp salt
¼ cup sugar
1 stick (8 tbsps) butter, chilled and diced, plus extra for greasing
½ cup whole milk
½ cup buttermilk (or to make your own, see p12)
2 tsp vanilla extract

### For the filling

15–20 large strawberries, hulled and halved
1 tbsp honey
1 cup heavy cream
¼ cup sugar

**1** Preheat the oven to 350°F (180°C). In a medium bowl, mix together the flour, cornmeal, baking powder, salt, and sugar. Add the butter to the flour mixture and work it into the dry ingredients with your hands, incorporating well, until the mixture resembles coarse breadcrumbs. Stir the milk, buttermilk, and 1 tsp vanilla extract into the dry ingredients and mix well.

**2** Grease the base and sides of a 12-hole muffin pan. Pour in the batter and bake in the oven for 35 minutes, or until golden brown. Remove and leave to cool slightly on a wire rack.

**3** For the filling, put the strawberries into a bowl, add the honey, and toss until well coated. Using an electric hand whisk or mixer, whisk the cream, sugar, and the remaining vanilla extract until stiff.

**4** Slice the shortcakes in half and fill each with whipped cream and strawberries. Serve warm.

# NOW TRY...

## FRESH BASIL

For a refreshing twist, toss the strawberries with honey and a handful of torn fresh **basil**.

## MANGO & LIME

Make a tropical shortcake by substituting the strawberries with 1 large diced **mango**, tossed in the juice of 1 **lime**.

## BERRIES & CREAM

Bake the shortcake batter in a greased 9in (23cm) round cake pan. Turn out the shortcake onto a large plate and top with 10oz (300g) **mixed berries**, 1 tbsp honey, and 1 cup **heavy cream**.

# CHOCOLATE-CRUSTED KEY LIME PIE

This pie takes its name from the small limes that grow in the Florida Keys, where the recipe originated.

★ **SERVES** 6-8
★ **PREP TIME** 20 mins
★ **COOK TIME** 15-20 mins, plus cooling

**Ingredients**

9oz (250g) chocolate graham crackers
⅓ cup sugar
9 tbsp unsalted butter, melted and cooled
5 limes
3 large egg yolks
14oz (400g) can condensed milk
cream, to serve

**1** Preheat the oven to 350°F (180°C). Crush the graham crackers in a plastic food bag with a rolling pin, or use a food processor. Mix the cracker crumbs and sugar with the butter in a large bowl until it resembles wet sand.

**2** Pour the cracker mixture into a 9in (23cm) loose-bottomed tart pan and press it firmly into the bottom and sides of the pan. Make sure the filling is packed as firmly as possible, and that there is a good side to the case so that the filling can be contained, unlike a cheesecake base. Place the tart pan on a baking sheet and bake for 10 minutes. Set aside to cool.

**3** Meanwhile, finely grate the zest of 3 limes into a bowl and, if you like, use a zester to pare long strands of zest from a fourth lime to decorate. Juice all 5 limes and set aside.

**4** Place the egg yolks into the bowl with the lime zest, and whisk with an electric whisk until the egg has thickened. Pour in the condensed milk and continue whisking for another 5 minutes. Add the lime juice and whisk again until it is incorporated. Pour the mixture into the pan and bake for 15–20 minutes, or until set but still wobbly in the center.

**5** Remove the pie from the oven and leave it to cool completely. Serve the pie decorated with the fine strands of lime zest, if using, and accompanied by cream.

**COOK'S TIP** A common baking mistake with deep-filled sweet tarts is to overcook them. Remove them from the oven when they still have a slight wobble to them at the center. They will cool and set to an unctuous, creamy texture. Overcooking will result in a tart with an unpleasantly "rubbery" texture.

**Key limes** have a distinct fragrance that sets them apart from their larger cousins, Persian limes.

# PECAN, MAPLE, AND BOURBON PIE

This sweet, crunchy pie originated in the South, where pecans are widely grown.

★ **SERVES** 6-8

★ **PREP TIME** 20 mins, plus chilling

★ **COOK TIME** 1 hr 20 mins, plus cooling

## Ingredients

1¼ cups all-purpose flour, plus extra for dusting
7 tbsp unsalted butter, chilled and diced
¼ cup sugar
1 egg yolk
½ tsp vanilla extract
whipped cream, to serve (optional)

## For the filling

⅔ cup maple syrup
4 tbsp butter
¾ cup light brown sugar
few drops of vanilla extract
pinch of salt
3 eggs
2 tbsp bourbon
1¾ cups pecans

**1** Using your fingertips, rub together the flour and butter, or pulse in a food processor until the mixture forms fine crumbs. Stir in the sugar. Beat the egg yolk with the vanilla and mix them into the dry ingredients, bringing the mixture together to form a soft dough. Add a little water to bring the dough together, if needed. Wrap in plastic wrap and chill for 1 hour. Preheat the oven to 350°F (180°C).

**2** Roll out the pastry on a well-floured surface to ⅛in (3mm) thick. It will be fragile, so if it begins to crumble, bring it together again with your hands and gently knead to get rid of any joins. Use it to line a 9in (23cm) loose-bottomed tart pan, leaving an overlapping edge of at least ¾in (2cm). Prick the base all over with a fork.

**3** Line the pastry case with parchment paper and weigh it down with baking beans. Place the case on a baking sheet and blind bake for 20 minutes. Remove the beans and paper, and bake for a further 5 minutes if the center still looks a little uncooked.

**4** For the filling, pour the maple syrup into a saucepan, and add the butter, sugar, vanilla extract, and salt. Place the pan over low heat, and stir constantly until the butter has melted and the sugar dissolved. Remove the pan from the heat and leave the mixture to cool until it feels just tepid, then beat in the eggs, one at a time, along with the bourbon. Stir in the pecan nuts, reserving enough for the top, then pour the mixture into the pastry case. Arrange the reserved pecans evenly across the top, pushing them in slightly.

**5** Bake for 40–50 minutes, or until just set. Cover with a sheet of foil if it is browning too quickly. Remove the pie from the oven, transfer to a wire rack, and leave to cool for 15–20 minutes. Remove from the pan and either serve it warm or leave it on the wire rack to cool completely. Serve with whipped cream, if desired.

# BOSTON CREAM TRIFLE

This rich trifle draws inspiration from the traditional Boston cream pie, with its luscious layers of cake and creamy custard.

★ **SERVES** 10

★ **PREP TIME** 45 mins, plus cooling and chilling

★ **COOK TIME** 45 mins, plus cooling

### Ingredients

1½ cup all-purpose flour
2 tsp baking powder
pinch of salt
1 stick (8 tbsps) butter, softened
¾ cup sugar
2 eggs, at room temperature
1 tsp vanilla extract
½ cup milk
1lb 5oz (600g) berries, such as blackberries, strawberries (hulled and halved), raspberries, and blueberries

### For the custard

1 cup milk
1 cup heavy cream
1 vanilla pod, split and seeds scraped
3 egg yolks
2 tbsp cornstarch
⅓ cup sugar
pinch of salt
1 tbsp unsalted butter, softened
1 tsp vanilla extract

### For the ganache

3 cups semisweet chocolate, broken into small pieces
1 cup heavy cream

**1** For the custard, heat the milk, cream, and vanilla pod in a saucepan over medium heat. Bring it to a simmer and remove from the heat immediately.

**2** In a medium bowl, whisk together the yolks, cornstarch, sugar, and salt. Gradually add the hot milk mixture, whisking constantly. Transfer to a clean saucepan and cook over low heat, stirring constantly, until the custard is thick enough to coat the back of a spoon. Sieve the custard into a bowl to remove the vanilla pod and any lumps. Stir in the butter and vanilla extract. Place a sheet of plastic wrap over the bowl, making sure it touches the top of the custard, and chill.

**3** Preheat the oven to 350°F (180°C). Double sift the flour, baking powder, and salt into a bowl and set aside. Using an electric hand whisk, cream together the butter and sugar in a separate bowl until light and fluffy. Add the eggs, one at a time, whisking between additions, then add the vanilla extract. Fold in the flour mixture using a large metal spoon, one-third at a time, alternating with the milk. Continue to fold until the batter is smooth and everything is well incorporated.

**4** Grease and line a 9in (23cm) square cake pan and pour the batter into the pan, making sure it spreads evenly. Bake for 25 minutes, or until golden brown and springy to the touch. Remove from the oven and let it cool.

**5** For the ganache, heat the chocolate and cream in a small heatproof bowl over a saucepan of simmering water (see technique for melting chocolate on p238). The bowl should not touch the water. Stir occasionally until the chocolate melts. Remove from the heat and set aside.

**6** Slice the cake into 5 x 5in (12 x 12cm) squares and place a layer of cake at the bottom of a tall glass bowl. Spread the berries evenly on top of the cake, reserving a handful for garnishing. Pour the custard evenly over the berries, then top with the remaining cake slices. Pour the ganache over the top and smooth it out. Top with the reserved berries and place in the fridge to chill. Serve chilled.

# LEMON AND GRAPEFRUIT MERINGUE PIE

An all-time classic dessert, the addition of grapefruit to the more usual lemon juice enhances the sweet and sour flavor.

★ **SERVES** 12
★ **PREP TIME** 25 mins, plus chilling
★ **COOK TIME** 1 hr

### For the pastry
1¼ cups all-purpose flour
2 tbsp sugar
pinch of salt
6 tbsp butter, chilled and cut into cubes
1 tbsp vegetable shortening

### For the filling
juice of 2 large lemons
juice of 1 small grapefruit
¾ cup sugar
½ cup cornstarch
5 egg yolks
1 tsp vanilla extract

### For the meringue
6 egg whites
3 tbsp sugar
¼ tsp vanilla extract
1 tsp cream of tartar

**1** For the pastry, sift the flour, sugar, and salt into a medium bowl and mix well to combine. Rub the butter and shortening into the flour mixture with your fingertips until it resembles breadcrumbs. Stir in ¼ cup of cold water and mix until a rough ball forms. Wrap in plastic wrap and chill for 1 hour.

**2** Preheat the oven to 350°F (180°C). Roll the pastry out on a floured work surface to fit the base of a lined 9in (23cm) square baking pan, gently pushing it into the edges to form a flat square. Bake for 30 minutes, or until golden brown. Remove from the oven and increase the temperature to 375°F (190°C).

**3** To make the filling, combine 2 cups of water, the lemon and grapefruit juice, sugar, and cornstarch in a saucepan over medium heat. Whisk for 2–3 minutes, until thickened. Put the egg yolks in a large bowl.

**4** Spoon the lemon and grapefruit mixture into the egg yolks, a little at a time, stirring well to incorporate. Return the filling to the pan and cook over medium heat for a further 5 minutes. Remove from the heat and add the vanilla extract. Stir in more lemon juice to taste, if necessary. Spread the filling evenly over the pie crust.

**5** For the meringue, whisk the egg whites, sugar, vanilla extract, and cream of tartar with an electric hand whisk on high speed until stiff peaks form.

**6** Use a pastry knife or large spoon to spread the meringue over the filling. Bake for 20 minutes, or until golden brown. Allow to cool completely before serving.

**Grapefruit**, an often overlooked citrus fruit, adds a complexity of flavor to lemon and lime dishes.

# MERINGUE-TOPPED SWEET POTATO PIE

Another classic and a close relative of the pumpkin pie, here a rich, sweet shortcrust is used for a truly crisp crust.

★ **SERVES** 6
★ **PREP TIME** 15 mins, plus chilling
★ **COOK TIME** 1½ hours

## Ingredients

1¼ cups all-purpose flour, plus extra for dusting
7 tbsp unsalted butter
¼ cup sugar
1 egg yolk
½ tsp vanilla extract

### For the filling

14oz (400g) sweet potato, peeled and chopped into small chunks
6 tbsp unsalted butter
½ cup muscovado sugar
3 tbsp half-and-half
1 egg
½ tsp ground nutmeg
½ tsp ground cinnamon
confectioners' sugar, for dusting

### For the meringue

3 egg whites, at room temperature
½ cup sugar
1 tsp cornstarch

**1** For the pastry, rub the flour and butter together in a bowl with your fingertips until the mixture resembles fine breadcrumbs. Stir in the sugar. Add the egg yolk and vanilla extract to the flour mixture and bring together to form a smooth dough, adding 1–2 teaspoons cold water, if needed. Wrap in plastic wrap and chill in the refrigerator for 30 minutes.

**2** For the filling, cook the sweet potato chunks in a saucepan of boiling water for 10–15 minutes, or until tender. Drain, return to the pan, and mash. Stir in the butter, sugar, cream, egg, and spices. Beat well to combine, then set aside.

**3** Preheat the oven to 350°F (180°C). Roll out the pastry on a floured surface to a round large enough to line a 8in (20cm) loose-bottomed tart pan. Place the pastry in the pan, pressing down well into the bottom and around the edges. Trim off any excess pastry, prick the bottom with a fork, and line with parchment paper. Place the pan on a baking sheet and fill with baking beans. Bake for 20 minutes. Remove the beans and paper and bake for a further 5 minutes if the center is uncooked.

**4** Spoon the filling into the pastry case and level with the back of a spoon. Bake for 35–45 minutes, or until the filling is set. Just before the filling is set, whisk the egg whites to stiff peaks. Whisk in the sugar and cornstarch.

**5** Remove the pie from the oven and spread the meringue over the top, making sure it is attached to the pastry on all sides (this will keep it from shrinking). Return the pie to the oven and cook for a further 10–15 minutes until the meringue is golden. Sprinkle with confectioners' sugar before serving.

# APPLE PIE

Thinly slicing the apples in this classic American pie gives the filling a soft, melting texture.

- ★ **SERVES** 6–8
- ★ **PREP TIME** 25 mins, plus chilling
- ★ **COOK TIME** 1 hr

### Ingredients
2⅓ cups all-purpose flour
⅓ cup sugar
13 tbsp unsalted
  butter, chilled

### For the filling
14oz (400g) Granny Smith
  (or other tart apples),
  peeled and cored weight
14oz (400g) Royal Gala
  (or other sweet apples),
  peeled and cored weight
2 tbsp lemon juice
3 tbsp all-purpose flour
4 tbsp sugar
4 tbsp light brown sugar
1 tsp ground cinnamon
1 egg, beaten with 1 tbsp
  cold water, for glazing

**Granny Smiths** are great for baking as they keep their texture once cooked.

**1** In a food processor or by hand, mix together the flour, sugar, and butter until the mixture resembles fine breadcrumbs. Add 5–6 tbsp of ice water and bring it together to form a soft dough. Wrap the pastry in plastic wrap and chill for 1 hour before using.

**2** Preheat the oven to 375°F (190°C). Remove the pastry from the fridge, cut off one-third, then rewrap the smaller piece and return it to the fridge.

**3** On a floured work surface, roll out the larger piece of pastry into a disk large enough to line a 9½in (24cm) pie dish. Lightly press the pastry into the dish and trim off any excess with a pair of scissors, allowing a ½in (1cm) overhang all around. Place in the fridge.

**4** Cut the apples into ¼in (5mm) slices and mix with the lemon juice in a large bowl until well combined. Sprinkle the flour, 3 tbsp of sugar, the brown sugar, and the cinnamon over the apples and toss them together so all the pieces are coated in the mixture.

**5** Pack the apples into the pie case, mounding the fruit slightly higher in the middle and ensuring it is well pressed down. Roll the reserved pastry into a disk large enough to fit the pie. Brush the edges of the pastry with a little egg wash, place the lid on top, and use your fingers to crimp the pieces of pastry together. Trim off any excess pastry with a small, sharp knife. Brush the top with egg wash, sprinkle with the remaining sugar, and cut 2 small slits in the top.

**6** Bake in the oven for 1 hour. (If using a ceramic or glass pie dish, place on a metal baking sheet to ensure the pastry bottom cooks thoroughly, extending the cooking time if necessary.) If the crust browns too early, cover it with foil, but remove it 5 minutes before the end of the cooking time to allow the top to remain crisp. Remove from the oven and leave to cool. Serve with vanilla ice cream or whipped cream.

## NOW TRY...

### GRUYÈRE & PEAR

Finely grate ¼ cup **Gruyère cheese** into the pastry at step 1 and use 1¾lb (800g) **Conference pears** insteac of the apples.

### STREUSEL TOPPING

Replace the pastry lid with a mixture of 2 tbsp each of **light brown sugar**, **all-purpose flour**, and **butter**, mixed to fine breadcrumbs with ¼ cup finely chopped **pecans** and 1 tsp **cinnamon**.

### SALTED CARAMEL

This sauce complements the pie perfectly. Gently heat a small jar of store-bought **caramel sauce** (to make your own, see p194) in a small, heavy-based saucepan, then whisk in ¼ cup **heavy cream** and a pinch of **sea salt flakes**.

# PECAN AND MAPLE PUMPKIN PIE

This version of the classic dessert produces a delicate, just-set pie, gently flavored with cinnamon and mixed spice.

- ★ **SERVES** 6–8
- ★ **PREP TIME** 30 mins, plus chilling
- ★ **COOK TIME** 1–1¼ hrs, plus cooling

### Ingredients

1¼ cup all-purpose flour, plus extra for dusting
7 tbsp unsalted butter, chilled and diced
¼ cup sugar
1 egg yolk
½ tsp vanilla extract

### For the filling

2½oz (75g) pecans, roughly chopped
3 eggs
½ cup light brown sugar
2 tsp ground cinnamon
1 tsp mixed spice
4 tbsp maple syrup
1¾ cups heavy cream
14oz can processed pumpkin, or 14oz (400g) roasted and puréed pumpkin

**1** To make the pastry, rub the flour and butter together in a large bowl with your fingertips until the mixture resembles breadcrumbs. Stir in the sugar. In a separate bowl, beat together the egg yolk and vanilla extract, then add to the flour mixture and bring the mixture together to form a soft dough, adding a little water if needed. Wrap in plastic wrap and chill for 30 minutes.

**2** Preheat the oven to 350°F (180°C). On a lightly floured surface, roll out the pastry to a thickness of ⅛in (3mm) and use it to line a 9in (23cm) loose-bottomed tart pan, leaving an overlapping edge of at least ¾in (2cm). Prick the bottom with a fork, line with parchment paper, and fill with baking beans.

**3** Place the pan on a baking tray and bake for 20 minutes. Remove the beans and parchment paper, and bake for a further 5 minutes if the center is uncooked. Sprinkle the pecans over the bottom of the pastry case.

**4** For the filling, whisk the eggs, brown sugar, half the cinnamon, the mixed spice, half the maple syrup, and half the cream together in a large bowl. When they are well blended, beat in the pumpkin to make a smooth filling. Partially pull out an oven rack from the oven and place the pan on it. Pour the filling into the case and slide the rack back into the oven.

**5** Bake for 45–50 minutes until the filling is set, but before it begins to bubble up at the edges. Trim off the pastry edge while still warm, then set the pie aside to cool in its pan for 15 minutes before turning out.

**6** Lightly whip the remaining cream until soft peaks start to form, stir in the remaining cinnamon and maple syrup, and serve with the pie.

**COOK'S TIP** The pie will keep for up to 2 days, chilled in an airtight container.

# LATTICE-TOPPED CHERRY PIE

The juice from the fruit is thickened with flour to help bring the filling together in this hugely popular pie.

★ **SERVES** 8

★ **PREP TIME** 40–45 mins, plus chilling

★ **COOK TIME** 20–25 mins

**Ingredients**

2 cups all-purpose flour, plus extra for dusting

½ tsp salt

½ cup shortening, chilled and diced

5 tbsp unsalted butter, chilled and diced

**For the filling and glaze**

1lb 2oz (500g) cherries, pitted (see technique, p242)

1 cup sugar, plus 1 tbsp for sprinkling

¼ cup all-purpose flour

¼ tsp almond extract (optional)

1 egg, beaten

**1** Sift together the flour and salt into a bowl. Rub the shortening and butter into the flour with your fingertips until crumbs begin to form. Sprinkle with 3 tbsp of water and blend until the dough turns into a ball. Wrap in plastic wrap and chill for 30 minutes.

**2** Preheat the oven to 400°F (200°C) and put in a baking sheet. On a floured surface, roll out two-thirds of the dough to a thickness of ⅛in (3mm) and use it to line a 9in (23cm) pie dish, leaving an overhang of at least ¾in (2cm). Press the dough into the dish and chill for 15 minutes.

**3** For the filling, put the cherries in a bowl and add the sugar, flour, and almond extract (if using). Mix well, then spoon into the case.

**4** Roll out the remaining dough into a rectangle. Cut out 12 strips, each ½in (1cm) wide, and arrange them in a latticelike pattern on top of the pie; trim the pastry. Use the beaten egg to glaze the lattice and secure the strips to the edge of the pie. Sprinkle the sugar over the top, place on the baking sheet, and bake for 20–25 minutes until the pastry is golden brown. Serve at room temperature or chilled.

# PEACH COBBLER

Gently poaching firmer peaches helps to break them down so that they cook more evenly.

★ **SERVES** 6-8
★ **PREP TIME** 25 mins
★ **COOK TIME** 30-35 mins

### Ingredients
¼ cup sugar
8 ripe peaches, peeled,
    pitted, and quartered
1 tsp cornstarch
juice of ½ lemon

### For the topping
2 cups self-rising flour
2 tsp baking powder
⅓ cup sugar
pinch of salt
½-¾ tsp ground cinnamon,
    to taste
5 tbsp unsalted butter
1 egg
½ cup buttermilk (or to
    make your own, see p12)
1 tbsp light brown sugar
ice cream, custard,
    or cream, to serve

**1** Preheat the oven to 375°F (190°C). For the filling, heat the sugar and 3–4 tbsp of water in a large, wide, heavy-based saucepan. Once the sugar has dissolved, add the quartered peaches, cover, and cook over medium heat for 2–3 minutes.

**2** In a small bowl, mix the cornstarch with the lemon juice to make a paste, then add it to the peaches. Continue to cook uncovered over low heat until the liquid thickens around the peaches. Transfer the peaches and syrup to a shallow ovenproof dish.

**3** To make the topping, sift the flour, baking powder, sugar, salt, and cinnamon into a large bowl. Rub in the butter with your fingertips until the mixture resembles fine breadcrumbs. Whisk together the egg and buttermilk in a separate bowl. Add the liquid to the dry ingredients and bring together to form a soft, sticky dough.

**4** Drop heaped tablespoons of the dough over the surface of the fruit, leaving a little space between them. Sprinkle with the sugar. Bake for 25–30 minutes until golden and bubbling. It is ready when a skewer inserted into the center of the topping comes out clean. Set aside to cool for 5 minutes before serving with ice cream, custard, or cream.

**Peaches**, cooked when just ripe, make their own thick, sweet sauce in this cobbler.

## NOW TRY...

### APPLE & BLACKBERRY

For an autumnal twist, replace the peaches with 2¼lb (1kg) **apples**, peeled, cored, and roughly chopped, along with 9oz (250g) **blackberries** to step 1 and cook as per the main recipe but bake for 40–45 minutes.

### QUICK SPICED PLUM

Toss 2¼lb (1kg) **plums**, pitted and halved, in ¼ cup light brown sugar along with 1 tsp cinnamon, ¼ tsp **nutmeg**, and ¼ tsp **allspice**. Place straight in the ovenproof dish and skip to step 3.

### PEACH & BLUEBERRY

For a Southern twist, add 5½oz (150g) **blueberries** to 6 prepared **peaches**. For the topping, replace ⅔ cups of the self-rising flour with an equal quantity of **fine polenta or cornmeal** and cook as usual.

# PINEAPPLE UPSIDE-DOWN CAKES WITH BASIL CREAM

## This classic dessert gets a gourmet makeover with the addition of a light, creamy sauce laced with basil.

★ **MAKES** 4
★ **PREP TIME** 20 mins
★ **COOK TIME** 40 mins

### Ingredients

3½ tbsp unsalted butter, plus extra for greasing
½ cup light brown sugar

### For the cakes

15oz (425g) can pineapple chunks in natural juice
5 tbsp unsalted butter, softened
½ cup sugar
2 eggs
½ tsp vanilla extract
1 cup self-rising flour

### For the pineapple and basil cream

1 cup juice from the canned pineapple
½ cup heavy cream
1 tsp finely chopped basil
1 tsp lime juice

**1** Melt the butter in a small, heavy-based saucepan over medium heat. Add the brown sugar and cook for 2–3 minutes, stirring constantly, until the sugar has dissolved. Divide the mixture between 4 large greased ramekins.

**2** Drain the pineapple and reserve the liquid. Take ⅔ cup of the pineapple and reserve the rest for another time. If the chunks are large, dice them first and then divide between the ramekins.

**3** Preheat the oven to 350°F (180°C). Using an electric hand whisk, cream the butter and sugar together in a bowl until light and fluffy. Beat in the eggs and vanilla extract until well combined. Sift in the flour and gently fold it in. Distribute the mixture evenly between the ramekins.

**4** Place the ramekins on a baking tray and bake in the center of the oven for 25–30 minutes, until well risen and golden brown, and a toothpick inserted into the center comes out clean.

**5** Meanwhile, pour the reserved pineapple juice into a small, heavy-based saucepan and bring to a boil. Cook for about 5 minutes, until it has reduced to ½ cup. Add half the cream and continue to reduce for a further 5–7 minutes, until you have only 3 tablespoons left. Remove from the heat and chill until needed.

**6** Remove the cakes from the oven and allow them to cool in the ramekins before placing them on serving plates. Leave the ramekins over the cakes for 2–3 minutes to ensure that all the syrup drips down into the cake.

**7** When you are ready to serve (they should be warm, but not too hot), mix the remaining cream into the chilled pineapple cream. Add the chopped basil and lime juice, and whisk together until thick. Serve alongside the warm cakes.

**COOK'S TIP** If the cakes have risen to a peak, cut off a little from the top to give a flatter finish to the cakes. This will enable them to stand up properly when turned out.

# BLUEBERRY RIPPLE CHEESECAKE

## The marbled effect on this cheesecake is simple to achieve and always looks impressive.

★ **SERVES** 8
★ **PREP TIME** 20 mins
★ **COOK TIME** 40 mins,
   plus cooling

### Ingredients

3½ tbsp unsalted butter,
   plus extra for greasing
4½oz (125g) graham crackers
5½oz (150g) blueberries
¾ cup sugar, plus 3 tbsp
1¾ cup cream cheese
1 cup mascarpone
2 large eggs, plus 1 large
   egg yolk
½ tsp vanilla extract
2 tbsp all-purpose flour, sifted

### For the compote

3½oz (100g) blueberries
1 tbsp sugar
squeeze of lemon

**1** Preheat the oven to 350°F (180°C). Grease the base and sides of a 8in (20cm) round deep springform cake pan. Put the crackers into a plastic food bag and crush with a rolling pin until they turn into fine crumbs.

**2** Melt the butter in a saucepan set over low heat; it should not begin to turn brown. Add the crumbs to the pan and stir until they are coated in butter. Remove from the heat. Press the crumbs into the base of the pan, pushing them down with the back of a spoon.

**3** Put the blueberries and 3 tbsp sugar in a food processor, and process until smooth. Push the mixture through a nylon sieve (metal will taint it) into a small saucepan. Bring to a boil, then simmer for 3–5 minutes, or until thickened and jammy. Set aside.

**4** Place the remaining sugar and the next 5 ingredients for the cheese mix in the processor. Process the cream cheese mixture until smooth and very well combined. Pour the mixture onto the cracker base and smooth the top with a palette knife. Drizzle over the berry jam and make swirls by drawing a metal skewer through the mix.

**5** Boil a few cups of water. Wrap the sides of the cake pan with tin foil and place in a deep roasting pan. Pour hot water into the pan, to come halfway up the cake pan; this prevents the mixture from cracking.

**6** Bake for 40 minutes until set but still a bit wobbly. Turn off the oven and wedge open the door. After 1 hour, remove the cake from the oven and place on a wire rack. Remove the sides of the pan. Slide 1 or 2 spatulas between the cracker base and the base of the pan. Transfer the cheesecake to a serving plate or cake stand, and leave to cool completely.

**7** Meanwhile, put all the ingredients for the compote in a small pan. Heat gently, stirring occasionally, until all the sugar dissolves. Transfer the compote to a small pitcher to serve.

**COOK'S TIP** The compote can be made 3 days in advance and chilled until needed.

# PEANUT BUTTER ICE CREAM SANDWICHES

Soft, rich chocolate cookies, salty peanut butter, and creamy vanilla ice cream—the perfect trio for the ultimate treat.

★ **MAKES** 4

★ **PREP TIME** 20 mins

★ **COOK TIME** 10 mins, plus cooling and freezing

### Ingredients

½ cup solid semisweet or dark chocolate (70 percent cocoa)

3½ tbsp unsalted butter

¼ cup sugar

¼ cup light brown sugar

1 egg

1 tbsp whole milk

1 tsp vanilla extract

1 cup all-purpose flour

4 tbsp crunchy peanut butter

4 scoops of good-quality vanilla ice cream (see p194)

**1** Preheat the oven to 350°F (180°C). Place the chocolate and butter in a heatproof bowl over a saucepan of simmering water, making sure the bowl does not touch the water (see technique for melting chocolate on p238). Stir constantly and remove the bowl from the heat as soon as the chocolate has melted. Set aside to cool.

**2** When the chocolate mixture has cooled, beat in the sugars, egg, milk, and vanilla extract. Sift in the flour and fold to combine. Place large tablespoons of the batter, spaced well apart, on 2 baking trays lined with parchment paper to make 8 large cookies. Bake in the center of the oven for 10 minutes, until just crispy at the edges but still soft in the middle. The cookies will firm up further as they cool.

**3** Leave the cookies to cool on the baking trays for 5 minutes before transferring them to a wire rack to cool completely, then put them in the freezer for 10 minutes before serving.

**4** To serve, spread the flat half of a cookie with a tablespoonful of the peanut butter. Spread the flat half of another (try to match up the sizes of the pairs of cookies) with a scoop of the vanilla ice cream, sandwich together, and serve immediately.

**COOK'S TIP** For an even richer cookie, add a handful of white or dark chocolate chips to the mixture before baking. You can even experiment with different ice cream flavors for the filling.

**Vanilla ice cream** is delicious served alone or as a cold, creamy contrast to a warm dessert.

# CARAMEL AND CHOCOLATE CRUNCH SUNDAE

A topping of salted caramel sauce and crunchy chocolate pretzels take this homemade vanilla ice cream to another level.

★ **SERVES** 4
★ **PREP TIME** 15 mins, plus chilling and churning
★ **COOK TIME** 20 mins

### Ingredients

2¼ cups heavy cream
2 cups whole milk
6 egg yolks
½ cup sugar
1 tsp vanilla extract
chocolate-covered pretzels
   (see p238)

### For the salted caramel sauce

1 cup sugar
1 stick (8 tbsps) butter, cut
   into cubes
½ cup heavy cream
1 tsp vanilla extract
1 tsp sea salt

**1** Heat the cream and milk in a heavy-based saucepan over medium heat, until hot but not boiling. In a separate bowl, whisk together the egg yolks, sugar, and vanilla extract. Very gradually, whisk the hot cream and milk into the egg mixture in a thin stream, whisking constantly.

**2** Return the custard to the rinsed-out pan and heat over medium heat, whisking constantly, until it thickens and just coats the back of a spoon. Do not heat it too fast or for too long, or the eggs will "scramble." Remove the custard from the heat and transfer to a clean, cold bowl immediately, whisking for a couple of minutes to cool it down.

**3** Cool the custard completely, then cover the surface with a layer of plastic wrap (placing it directly on the custard) to prevent a skin forming. Transfer to the fridge and chill for a minimum of 4 hours, or overnight.

**4** Pour the chilled custard into an ice-cream maker and churn it until it is a thick, scoopable ice cream. Transfer it to a plastic container and freeze until needed.

**5** To prepare the salted caramel sauce, melt the sugar in a heavy-based frying pan over medium heat. As it melts, whisk frequently for 7–10 minutes, until it becomes amber brown. Add the butter and whisk to combine.

**6** Remove from the heat and add the cream. Continue whisking as the caramel bubbles, until it settles into a smooth mixture. Whisk in the vanilla extract and sea salt. Set aside to cool completely.

**7** To serve, roughly crush some chocolate-covered pretzels from p238 in a plastic food bag and scatter over the ice cream. Finish with a drizzle of the salted caramel sauce.

**COOK'S TIP** For a healthier version, try a spoonful of the Fresh berry compote with vanilla and thyme from p242 or the dried fruit compote from p60, and top with a handful of fresh blueberries.

# APPLE DUMPLINGS WITH VANILLA ICE CREAM

Simple to make, these individual apple dumplings look amazing on a plate. Serve with store-bought ice cream if time is short.

- ★ **MAKES** 4
- ★ **PREP TIME** 25 mins, plus chilling
- ★ **COOK TIME** 45 mins

**Ingredients**

4 Golden Delicious apples, peeled and cored
4 tbsp butter
1 tsp ground cinnamon, plus extra for coating
1 egg, beaten
2 tbsp light brown sugar

**For the pastry**

2½ cups all-purpose flour, plus extra for dusting
1 tsp salt
3 tbsp sugar
¾ cup butter, chilled and cut into cubes
¼ cup vegetable shortening

**For the ice cream**

1 cup whole milk
1 cup heavy cream
1 vanilla pod, split
4 egg yolks
½ cup light brown sugar
1 tsp ground cinnamon
Salted caramel sauce, to serve

**1** First, make the ice cream. In a saucepan, whisk together the milk and cream, and add the vanilla pod. Let it simmer for 20 minutes on low heat. Remove from the heat and discard the vanilla pod.

**2** In a separate saucepan, whisk together the egg yolks, sugar, and cinnamon. Spoon the cream mixture into the eggs, a little at a time, and whisk until well combined. Simmer on low heat for 10–12 minutes, or until thickened. Transfer to a bowl, cover, and chill for 1 hour, or until thoroughly chilled.

**3** To make the pastry, combine the flour, salt, and sugar in a bowl. Rub the butter and shortening into the flour mixture with your fingertips until it resembles breadcrumbs. Stir in ¼ cup of cold water to form a soft dough. Wrap in plastic wrap and chill for 1 hour.

**4** Pour the cream mixture into an ice-cream maker and churn it for 20–30 minutes, depending on the machine, or until creamy and firm. Transfer it to an airtight container and freeze for at least 30 minutes.

**5** Preheat the oven to 325°F (160°C). Divide the dough into 4 equal pieces. Roll them out on a floured work surface to form 6in (15cm) rounds. Wrap each disk around an apple. Fill each apple core with a tbsp of butter and ¼ tsp of cinnamon, and pinch the dough closed around the apple. Transfer the apples to a 9in (23cm) square baking sheet.

**6** Brush each apple with the egg and sprinkle over the brown sugar and a little cinnamon. Bake for 45 minutes, or until the pastry is golden and the apple has softened. Serve each apple hot with a scoop of ice cream and a drizzle of Salted caramel sauce (see p194).

# SPICED APPLE AND PEAR CRISP

Give a simple apple crisp an autumnal twist with juicy pears and gentle spicing.

★ **SERVES** 4–6
★ **PREP TIME** 20 mins
★ **COOK TIME** 35 mins

**Ingredients**

2 tbsp butter
3 apples, peeled and
   thickly sliced
3 pears, peeled and
   thickly sliced
2 tbsp light brown sugar
pinch of ground cinnamon
pinch of ground ginger
juice of 1 lemon
vanilla ice cream, to serve

**For the topping**

1 cup rolled oats
1¼ cups all-purpose flour
1 cup light brown sugar
8 tbsps (1 stick) butter, melted
1 tsp ground cinnamon
pinch of salt

**1** Preheat the oven to 350°F (180°C). Melt the butter in a large saucepan over low heat. Add the apples, pears, sugar, cinnamon, ginger, and lemon juice. Simmer over medium-low heat, stirring occasionally, for 6–8 minutes, or until the apples and pears have browned and softened slightly.

**2** Meanwhile, mix together the oats, flour, sugar, butter, cinnamon, and salt in a bowl. Spoon the fruit mixture into the bottom of a 8in (20cm) round flameproof casserole. Top with the oat mixture, spreading it evenly.

**3** Bake in the oven for 30–35 minutes, or until golden brown and bubbling. Serve hot with vanilla ice cream on the side.

**Apples and pears**, the quintessential fruits of fall, will keep for months when stored at a low, constant temperature.

# COCONUT FUNNEL CAKES

Often served at fairs and amusement parks, these coconut-infused funnel cakes make a delicious homemade treat.

★ **MAKES** 4-6
★ **PREP TIME** 10 mins
★ **COOK TIME** 25 mins

### Ingredients

2 eggs
1 cup whole milk
1 cup coconut milk
2 cups all-purpose flour
1 tsp vanilla extract
4 tbsp sugar
2 tbsp baking powder
pinch of salt
2 cups coconut
  or vegetable oil
confectioners' sugar, to decorate
shaved coconut, to decorate

**1** Whisk together the eggs, milk, and coconut milk. Add the flour, vanilla extract, sugar, baking powder, and salt. Stir well to combine and transfer to a plastic food bag.

**2** In a large, heavy-based saucepan or deep-fat fryer, heat the oil to 375°F (190°C) as shown in the technique on p144. When the oil is hot enough, snip a hole in one corner of the bag and squeeze a portion of the batter into the pan, making a swirling shape in a circular motion. Fry for 2–3 minutes on each side, or until both sides are golden brown.

**3** Remove from the oil with tongs and drain on a wire rack. Repeat with the remaining batter to make the rest of the cakes. Decorate with sifted confectioners' sugar and shaved coconut. Serve hot.

**Coconut products**, such as milk, oil, and dried coconut itself, each have their own distinctive taste and uses in the kitchen.

# BAKING, CANDY, AND PRESERVES

# PECAN CARAMEL CINNAMON BUNS

Sweet, sticky, and oozing with homemade caramel, these cinnamon buns are perfect for a sumptuous weekend brunch.

★ **MAKES** 9
★ **PREP TIME** 40 mins, plus rising
★ **COOK TIME** 30 mins

**Ingredients**
2¼ tsp (7g) sachet active dried yeast
½ cup sugar
½ cup whole milk
1 stick (8 tbsps) butter
pinch of salt
1 egg
3½ cups all-purpose flour, plus extra for dusting
vegetable oil, for greasing

**For the caramel sauce**
1 cup light brown sugar
1 stick (8 tbsps) butter, cut into cubes
1 tsp vanilla extract
½ cup heavy cream

**For the filling**
1 stick (8 tbsps) butter
¼ cup light brown sugar
1 tbsp ground cinnamon
1 cup chopped pecans

**For the icing**
1 cup confectioners' sugar
1 tbsp whole milk

**1** Dissolve the yeast in ¼ cup warm water with a pinch of sugar. Set aside for 5–7 minutes, or until it begins to bubble. In a saucepan, heat the milk and butter over low heat until the butter has melted. Remove immediately from the heat. In a medium bowl, mix the yeast mixture, the remaining sugar, salt, egg, the melted butter mixture, and half the flour. Stir to incorporate, then add the remaining flour, until the mixture comes together to form a dough.

**2** Knead the dough for 5 minutes, adding flour as necessary so that the dough is not sticky. Put it in an oiled bowl, cover with plastic wrap, and keep in a warm place for 1 hour until well risen.

**3** Meanwhile, make the caramel sauce. In a heavy-based frying pan, melt the sugar, stirring constantly with a whisk. The sugar will clump, but continue to stir. Once the sugar has melted and reached a dark brown color, add the butter. Continue to stir as the butter melts and incorporates. Add the vanilla extract and cream, and continue stirring until the boiling has stopped. Remove from the heat and let it cool.

**4** Preheat the oven to 350°F (180°C). Place the dough onto a floured surface and roll it out to a thickness of ½in (1cm). To make the filling, melt the butter and mix with the sugar, cinnamon, and pecans. Spread the filling evenly over the dough. Roll the dough up to form a tight spiral.

**5** Pour the caramel sauce into a 9 x 9in (23 x 23cm) baking pan. Cut the dough roll into 9 equal slices and press into the caramel sauce. Bake for 25–30 minutes, or until the buns are golden brown and the caramel is bubbling. The center of the buns should remain slightly gooey and undercooked. Whisk together the confectioners' sugar and milk and pour the icing over the hot buns. Serve hot.

# CHOCOLATE AND CHERRY DEVIL'S FOOD CAKE

This classic uses kirsch to enhance the richness of the chocolate, adding a wonderful depth of flavor to the cake.

- ★ **SERVES** 8-10
- ★ **PREP TIME** 30 mins
- ★ **COOK TIME** 30–35 mins, plus cooling

## Ingredients

7 tbsp unsalted butter, softened, plus extra for greasing
1⅓ cups sugar
2 large eggs
1⅔ cups self-rising flour
1 cup cocoa powder
1 tsp baking powder
¼ cup kirsch
¾ cup whole milk
1 tsp vanilla extract

## For the icing

11 tbsps unsalted butter, cut into cubes
⅓ cup cocoa powder
1⅓ cups confectioners' sugar
¼ cup whole milk
1 small can cherries, drained and roughly chopped
scant 1oz (25g) dark chocolate, to garnish

**1** Preheat the oven to 350°F (180°C). Grease two 8in (20cm) round cake pans and line the bases with parchment paper. In a medium bowl, use an electric whisk to cream together the butter and sugar until light and fluffy.

**2** Beat in the eggs one at a time, whisking well after each addition. In a separate bowl, sift together the flour, cocoa powder, and baking powder. In another bowl, mix together the kirsch, milk, and vanilla extract.

**3** Beat alternate spoonfuls of the dry and liquid ingredients into the cake batter. Once the mixture is well blended, divide it evenly between the two pans.

**4** Bake for 30–35 minutes until the cakes are springy to the touch and a skewer inserted into the center comes out clean. Leave to cool in the pans for a few minutes, then turn out onto a wire rack to cool completely. Remove the parchment paper.

**5** For the icing, melt the butter in a frying pan over low heat. Add the cocoa powder and continue to cook for a minute or two, stirring frequently. Allow to cool completely.

**6** Sift in the confectioners' sugar, beating thoroughly to combine. Blend in the milk, 1 tbsp at a time, until smooth and glossy. Allow to cool (it will thicken) and then mix half the icing with the cherries and use to sandwich the cakes together. Decorate the top and sides of the cake with the remaining half of the icing. Finally, use a vegetable peeler to create chocolate shavings and scatter them evenly over the top of the cake.

**COOK'S TIP** This cake will keep in an airtight container in a cool place for up to 5 days.

# ANGEL FOOD CAKE WITH BLACKBERRY SAUCE

This show-stopping sponge cake, made without the addition of butter or oil, is as light as air.

★ **SERVES** 8

★ **PREP TIME** 20 mins

★ **COOK TIME** 35 mins, plus cooling

## Ingredients

1¼ cups sugar

1 tsp salt

¾ cup super-fine flour or twice-sifted all-purpose flour (see Cook's tip, right)

12 large eggs, at room temperature, separated

2 tsp vanilla extract

whipped cream, to serve

## For the blackberry sauce

12oz (350g) blackberries

1 cup honey

juice of 1 lemon

**1** Heat the oven to 350°F (180°C). In a food processor, process the sugar and salt until very fine. Sift the flour and half the sugar mixture into a bowl and set aside.

**2** Put the egg whites in another bowl and add the vanilla extract. Using an electric hand whisk or mixer, whisk for 5 minutes, or until the egg whites are stiff. Add the remaining sugar mixture, a little at a time, and keep beating so that the mixture remains stiff.

**3** Add the flour and sugar mix into the egg mixture and fold it in with a rubber spatula. When well incorporated, spoon the batter into a non-greased 10in (25cm) bundt pan, and bake for 35 minutes. Allow the cake to cool for 1 hour in the pan.

**4** Meanwhile, put the blackberries, honey, and lemon juice in a nonreactive saucepan (not aluminum or cast-iron) and cook over low heat. Simmer, stirring continuously, until the blackberries break down. Set aside to cool.

**5** To serve, turn the cake out onto a plate. Slice, spoon over the blackberry sauce, and serve with freshly whipped cream.

**COOK'S TIP** If using all-purpose flour, sift it twice to produce a very light cake. For the best result, lift the sieve high above the bowl, allowing the flour to come into contact with as much air as possible, as it floats down.

**Blackberries** are soft fruits that freeze well. Frozen ones can be used as a substitute when cooking.

# DOUBLE CHOCOLATE BROWNIES

Brownies are better when slightly undercooked, as they retain their moist interior and store better, too.

- ★ **MAKES** 16-20
- ★ **PREP TIME** 15 mins
- ★ **COOK TIME** 40 mins, plus cooling

### Ingredients

8 tbsp butter, melted, plus extra for greasing
½ cup sugar
½ cup light brown sugar
4 eggs
1 tsp vanilla extract
¾ cup all-purpose flour
1½ cups cocoa powder
¼ tsp baking soda
8oz (225g) dark chocolate chips

**1** Preheat the oven to 300°F (150°C). Using an electric hand whisk or mixer, combine the butter, sugars, eggs, and vanilla extract in a large bowl until well mixed.

**2** In a separate bowl, combine the flour, cocoa powder, and baking soda. Stir the flour mixture into the butter mixture, one-third at a time, making sure that it is well incorporated before each addition. Mix in the chocolate chips.

**3** Grease and line a 9 x 9in (23 x 23cm) baking tray or brownie pan and spoon the batter into it. Use a spatula to spread the batter evenly, ensuring the corners are filled.

**4** Bake for 35–40 minutes, or until cooked through and firm. Remove from the oven and leave the brownie to cool in the pan, then turn out of the pan and cut into 16–20 squares.

**Dark chocolate chips** are a must in any cook's pantry for those last-minute baking projects.

## NOW TRY...

### CHERRY & WALNUT

For nutty brownies, substitute the chocolate chips with ½ cup **dried cherries** and 1 cup **crushed walnuts**. Add to the batter and distribute evenly.

### PEANUT BUTTER

Spoon 1 cup **smooth peanut butter** over half the batter and top with the rest of the batter to create a rich middle layer. Then bake as directed in step 4.

### BUTTERSCOTCH

Try replacing the chocolate chips with the same quantity of **butterscotch pieces**.

# PUMPKIN PIE SPICE BEIGNETS

Popular in New Orleans, these fritters are believed to have been brought to Louisiana by French settlers in the 18th century.

- ★ **MAKES** 40
- ★ **PREP TIME** 20 mins, plus rising and chilling
- ★ **COOK TIME** 20 mins

### Ingredients

2¼ tsp (7g) sachet active dried yeast

1 cup heavy cream

½ stick (4 tbsps) butter

½ cup sugar

2 eggs

5 cups all-purpose flour, plus extra for dusting

1¾ pints (1 liter) peanut or sunflower oil, for frying

### For the pumpkin pie spice

1 tbsp ground cinnamon

½ tbsp ground ginger

½ tbsp ground nutmeg

½ tbsp ground cloves

½ cup confectioners' sugar

**1** Dissolve the yeast in ½ cup warm water with a pinch of sugar. Leave to stand for 5–7 minutes, or until it begins to bubble.

**2** In a saucepan, heat the cream and butter over low heat until the butter has melted. Remove immediately from the heat. In a large bowl, mix the sugar, eggs, yeast mixture, and the melted butter and cream. Add half the flour and stir to incorporate. Gradually add the remaining flour, one-third at a time, until the mixture comes together to form a large ball of dough.

**3** Knead the dough for 5–7 minutes, adding flour as needed so that the dough is not sticky. Form the dough into a ball and place in a covered bowl or freezer bag. Chill for 4–6 hours until doubled in size. Put the dough onto a floured surface and roll it out to a thickness of ½in (1cm). Cut into 1½in (4cm) squares.

**4** To make the pumpkin pie spice, mix together the cinnamon, ginger, nutmeg, cloves, and confectioners' sugar in a small bowl.

**5** In a large, heavy-based saucepan or deep-fat fryer, heat the oil to 375°F (190°C), as shown in the technique on p144. Fry the squares, 5 or 6 at a time, for 1–2 minutes on each side, or until golden brown and puffed. Remove with a slotted spoon and transfer to a wire rack to cool.

**6** Using a sieve or fine mesh strainer, sprinkle over the spice mixture and serve hot. For a true New Orleans experience, try these delicious desserts with a cup of coffee blended with chicory.

**Nutmeg** gives a sweet spiciness and delicate warmth to sweet and savory dishes.

# RED VELVET CUPCAKES

These fashionable cupcakes taste great and, with red-toned cake against a pale, buttery cream cheese frosting, look beautiful, too.

- ★ **MAKES** 18–20
- ★ **PREP TIME** 25 mins
- ★ **COOK TIME** 22–25 mins, plus cooling

### Ingredients

9 tbsp unsalted butter, softened
1¼ cup sugar
2 eggs, lightly beaten
2 tsp red food coloring
1 tsp vanilla extract
2 cups self-rising flour
4 tbsp cocoa powder
1 cup buttermilk (or to make your own, see p12)
1 tsp apple cider vinegar
1 tsp baking soda

### For the frosting

¼ cup cream cheese
3½ tbsp unsalted butter, softened
1¾ cups confectioners' sugar
1 tsp vanilla extract

**1** Preheat the oven to 350°F (180°C). Place the butter and sugar in a large bowl. Using an electric hand whisk, cream them together until the mixture is very light and fluffy. Whisk in the eggs, food coloring, and vanilla extract until they are well combined.

**2** Sift together the flour and cocoa powder. Add one-third of the flour to the cake batter and whisk it in well. Add half of the buttermilk and whisk it again, then another one-third of the flour, the rest of the buttermilk, and the final one-third of the flour, making sure to whisk well between additions. Mix together the apple cider vinegar and baking soda in a separate bowl and quickly fold into the batter.

**3** Place 18–20 cupcake liners in two deep, 12-hole muffin pans (they will help the cupcakes keep their shape). Spoon the batter into the liners, filling each two-thirds full. Bake for 22–25 minutes, until springy to the touch. Do not open the oven until at least 20 minutes of baking time has passed. Transfer to a wire rack to cool completely.

**4** To make the frosting, beat the cream cheese, butter, confectioners' sugar, and vanilla extract until light and creamy, and transfer to a piping bag fitted with a star-shaped nozzle (if using).

**5** Pipe the frosting onto the cupcakes, or if frosting by hand, use the back of a spoon dipped in warm water to smooth the surface of each cake.

**COOK'S TIP** The cupcakes can be made up to 1 day ahead and stored, unfrosted, in an airtight container. They are best frosted on the day they are to be eaten.

# STRAWBERRIES AND CREAM WHOOPIE PIES

Best served immediately, these strawberry-layered whoopie pies make a lovely addition to a summer party.

- ★ **MAKES** 10
- ★ **PREP TIME** 40 mins
- ★ **COOK TIME** 12 mins

## Ingredients

1½ sticks (¾ cup) unsalted butter, softened
¾ cup light brown sugar
1 large egg
1 tsp vanilla extract
1¾ cups self-rising flour
1 cup cocoa powder
1 tsp baking powder
¾ cup whole milk
2 tbsp Greek yogurt or thick plain yogurt
¾ cup heavy cream, whipped
9oz (250g) strawberries, hulled and thinly sliced
confectioners' sugar, for dusting

**1** Preheat the oven to 350°F (180°C). Line several baking sheets with parchment paper. Using an electric hand whisk, cream the butter and sugar until fluffy. Beat in the egg and vanilla extract. In a bowl, sift together the flour, cocoa, and baking powder. Mix the dry ingredients and the milk into the batter alternately, a spoonful at a time. Fold in the yogurt.

**2** Put heaped tablespoons of the batter onto the baking sheets, leaving space for the mixture to spread. Dip a tablespoon in warm water and use the back to smooth over the surface of the cakes.

**3** Bake for 12 minutes, until well risen. Leave the cakes for a few minutes, then turn out onto a wire rack to cool.

**4** Spread the cream onto the flat side of half of the cakes. Top with a layer of strawberries and a second cake. Dust with confectioners' sugar and serve. These pies do not store and should be eaten on the day.

# TRIPLE-LAYERED COCONUT CAKE

There is something very indulgent about a triple-layered cake, and this one, stuffed with whipped cream, is no exception!

★ **SERVES** 8–10

★ **PREP TIME** 30 mins

★ **COOK TIME** 35 mins, plus cooling

## Ingredients

1 cup (2 sticks) butter, softened, plus extra for greasing

2 cups sugar

½ cup coconut oil

2 tsp vanilla extract

4 eggs, at room temperature

4 egg whites, at room temperature

3½ cups all-purpose flour, plus extra for dusting

½ tsp salt

1 tbsp baking powder

1½ cups coconut milk

½ cup shredded coconut, to decorate

### For the whipped cream

2 cups heavy cream

¼ cup sugar

1 tsp vanilla extract

**1** Preheat the oven to 350°F (180°C). Using an electric hand whisk or a mixer, cream together the butter, sugar, and oil. Beat in the vanilla extract, and then the eggs, one at a time. Once the eggs are fully incorporated, beat in the egg whites until light and fluffy.

**2** Sift together the flour, salt, and baking powder into a bowl. Add to the egg mixture, one-third at a time, alternating with the coconut milk. Beat together until fully incorporated and the mixture is light and fluffy.

**3** Grease three 9in (23cm) round cake pans and lightly dust them with flour. Divide the batter evenly between the pans. Bake for 30–35 minutes, or until a toothpick inserted into the center comes out clean. Allow the cakes to cool for 10 minutes in the pan before transferring to a wire rack to cool completely.

**4** Toss the shredded coconut in a frying pan over medium heat until toasted. For the whipped cream, whip the cream, sugar, and vanilla extract until stiff.

**5** Place one cake on a plate and spread one-third of the whipped cream over it. Place the second cake over the cream and spread another one-third of the cream. Then top with the third cake and spread over the remaining cream. Sprinkle with the toasted coconut and serve.

# CHOCOLATE FUDGE CUPCAKES

These decidedly grown up cupcakes are truly decadent topped with a rich, dark chocolate ganache and fresh raspberries.

- ★ **MAKES** 12
- ★ **PREP TIME** 30 mins
- ★ **COOK TIME** 20 mins, plus cooling

### Ingredients

½ cup cocoa powder
⅔ cup semisweet or dark chocolate
8 tbsps (1 stick) butter, softened
1 cup sugar
3 eggs, at room temperature
1 cup all-purpose flour
1 tsp baking soda
2 tsp baking powder
pinch of salt
½ cup whole milk
raspberries, to garnish

### For the ganache

2½ cups semisweet or dark chocolate
1½ cups heavy cream

**1** Preheat the oven to 350°F (180°C). In a small saucepan, heat the cocoa, chocolate, and ¾ cup of water over low heat. Whisk together until fully incorporated.

**2** Using an electric hand whisk, cream together the butter and sugar in a large bowl until light and fluffy. Add the eggs, one at a time, beating thoroughly between each addition. Whisk this into the chocolate mixture. In another bowl, sift the flour, baking soda, baking powder, and salt.

**3** Add the dry ingredients to the chocolate mixture in thirds, alternating with the milk. Beat until the mixture is light and well blended. Place 12 cupcake cases into a 12-hole muffin pan. Spoon the batter into the cases, filling each two-thirds full.

**4** Bake for 17–20 minutes, or until a toothpick inserted into the center of a cupcake comes out clean. Transfer the cupcakes to a wire rack to cool.

**5** To make the ganache, melt the chocolate and cream in a small heatproof bowl over a saucepan of simmering water, making sure the bowl does not touch the water (see technique for melting chocolate on p238). When the chocolate has melted, take it off the heat and whisk until smooth and completely combined. Set aside.

**6** When the ganache returns to room temperature, whip until fluffy. Let it chill, then spoon onto the cupcakes. Garnish with raspberries and serve.

**Raspberries**, with their sweet yet tart flavor, pair well with rich, dark chocolate.

# BLUEBERRY COFFEE CAKE

Here, the sweet, crumbly streusel topping is enhanced with little nuggets of pecans for extra crunch.

★ **SERVES** 16
★ **PREP TIME** 20 mins
★ **COOK TIME** 50 mins

## Ingredients

8 tbsps (1 stick) butter, plus
   extra for greasing
¾ cup light
   brown sugar
1 tsp vanilla extract
2 eggs
1½ cups all-purpose flour,
   plus 2 tbsp for tossing
pinch of salt
½ tsp baking powder
½ tsp baking soda
1 cup milk
9oz (250g) blueberries

## For the topping

4 tbsps butter, melted
½ cup all-purpose flour
½ cup light brown sugar
1 cup chopped pecans
1 tsp ground ginger
1 tsp ground cinnamon

**1** Preheat the oven to 350°F (180°C). Using an electric hand whisk, cream together the butter and sugar until light and fluffy. Add the vanilla extract and eggs, one at a time, whisking well between each addition.

**2** Sift the flour, salt, baking powder, and baking soda into a bowl. Fold into the butter mixture, a little at a time, alternating with the milk. Stir to combine.

**3** In a separate bowl, toss the blueberries with 2 tbsp of flour, then fold them into the mixture. Scoop the batter into a greased 9 x 14in (23 x 35cm) baking pan and spread evenly.

**4** For the topping, mix together the butter, flour, sugar, pecans, and spices. Sprinkle over the batter. Bake for 45–50 minutes, or until the cake has risen, and a skewer inserted into the center comes out clean. Serve hot with a cup of coffee.

# A taste of the PACIFIC NORTHWEST

ALASKA

## FOODS AND FLAVORS

★ The **geoduck**, a giant clam that can live for up to 150 years and weighs more than 10lb (4.5kg), is a local delicacy, as well as being popular in Japanese cuisine.

★ The many **berries** of the area, including huckleberries, yellow raspberries, and boysenberries, are used in a variety of pies, preserves, and compotes (see below).

★ **Salmon**, pulled from the cold, deep waters of the Pacific, is often smoked on cedar planks to enhance its rich, full flavor.

★ **Apples** are just one of the fruits widely produced here, and many varieties can be found in local farmers' markets.

★ Seattle's **Pike Place Market** is rightly famous for its fresh local produce, and as the best place to buy fish straight from the sea.

With some of the longest coastlines in the country and a cool, wet climate, the states of the Pacific Northwest are renowned for their seafood and for the rich bounty of the land.

The Pacific Northwest was one of the last regions of the US to be colonized, with the first sizeable group of immigrants not settling the region until the 1840s. They arrived to find high mountains, fertile valleys, an abundance of wild game and berries, and the shorelines and rivers full of salmon and trout. In fact, some of the best fishing in the country is found in far-flung Alaska, where the Pacific salmon is highly prized.

As a more recently established cuisine, the food here is less clearly defined than it is, say, in the Southeast, with the character of a dish often coming from the quality of the local ingredients rather than any one style. However, the influence of centuries-old Native American cuisine can still be seen and, in recent years, the local Asian community has introduced its own distinctive flavors.

*Pike Place Market is one of the longest-running farmers' markets in the country, dating back to 1907.*

**Alaskan King crabs are a classic local catch. Some of these giant crustaceans can grow legs measuring an incredible 6ft (1.8m) in length.**

salmon is perhaps the best-known Alaskan export, and one of which it can be justly proud.

ALASKA
EWC 630
THE LAST FRONTIER

All around the San Francisco Bay area, local versions of cioppino, the seafood stew, can be found.

The coastlines of the Pacific Northwest, especially those around Big Sur, are known for their rugged, natural beauty.

seattle has a good claim for being the birthplace of the modern coffee culture.

Fresh, seared tuna steaks give a classic tuna spaghetti casserole a modern makeover.

# CHOCOLATE ZUCCHINI BUNDT CAKE

Zucchini can be used in the same way as carrots in carrot cake. The grated vegetables keep the cake moist for days.

★ **SERVES** 6–8
★ **PREP TIME** 20 mins
★ **COOK TIME** 55 mins

**Ingredients**

8 tbsps (1 stick) butter, softened, plus extra for greasing
¼ cup coconut oil
1 cup sugar
1 cup light brown sugar
½ tsp vanilla extract
2 eggs, at room temperature
2 cups all-purpose flour
2 tsp baking powder
½ cup cocoa powder
pinch of salt
14oz (400g) zucchini, grated
confectioners' sugar, for dusting

**1** Preheat the oven to 325°F (160°C). Using an electric hand whisk, beat together the butter, oil, sugars, and vanilla extract in a large bowl. Add the eggs, one at a time, whisking well between each addition.

**2** Sift together the flour, baking powder, cocoa, and salt into a bowl. Add to the butter mixture, a little at a time, beating in until well combined.

**3** Using a rubber spatula, fold the grated zucchini into the batter, stirring well so that it is fully incorporated and well coated.

**4** Scoop the batter into a greased 9in (23cm) bundt pan and bake for 45–55 minutes, or until a toothpick inserted into the center comes out clean. Using a sieve or fine mesh strainer, lightly dust the cake with confectioners' sugar. Serve warm.

**COOK'S TIP** If you don't have a bundt pan, you can easily make your own with a 10in (25cm) round cake pan and a small dariole mold or ramekin. Grease as usual and fill the mold with baking beans to hold it in place in the middle of the pan. Then pour the batter around it.

**Zucchini** has a subtle flavor, so it will not overwhelm this sweet treat.

# LEMON SOUR CREAM POUND CAKE

Replacing some of the butter with sour cream keeps the pound cake moist, and the lemons add a nice, tart flavor.

★ **SERVES** 8-10
★ **PREP TIME** 20 mins
★ **COOK TIME** 45 mins, plus cooling

## Ingredients

1 cup butter, softened, plus extra for greasing
2 cups sugar
6 eggs
1 tsp vanilla extract
3 cups all-purpose flour
¼ tsp baking soda
1 cup sour cream

### For the glaze

1 tbsp whole milk
juice of 1 lemon
1 cup confectioners' sugar

**1** Preheat the oven to 350°F (180°C). Using an electric hand whisk, beat the butter in a large bowl and gradually add the sugar, beating until light and fluffy. Add the eggs, one at a time, whisking well between each addition. Beat in the vanilla extract.

**2** Sift together the flour and baking soda into a bowl. Add to the egg mixture, one-third at a time, alternating with the sour cream.

**3** Spoon the batter into a greased fluted 10in (25cm) round cake pan or bundt pan (or see Cook's Tip, opposite). Bake for 40–45 minutes, or until golden brown and firm. Allow the cake to cool for 10 minutes before turning it out onto a serving plate.

**4** For the glaze, whisk together the milk, lemon juice, and sugar. Slowly pour the glaze evenly over the cake. Serve warm.

# CHOCOLATE CHIP COOKIES

These easy-to-make cookies are soft and chewy, and incredibly delicious.

- ★ **MAKES** 15
- ★ **PREP TIME** 10 mins
- ★ **COOK TIME** 15 mins, plus cooling

**Ingredients**

7 tbsp unsalted butter, softened
½ cup sugar
½ cup light brown sugar
1 large egg
1 tsp vanilla extract
1½ cups all-purpose flour
½ tsp baking powder
½ tsp salt
¾ cup milk chocolate chips

**1** Preheat the oven to 350°F (180°C). In a large bowl, cream together the butter and sugars with an electric hand whisk until light and fluffy. Beat in the egg and vanilla extract.

**2** Sift together the flour, baking powder, and salt and mix into the wet mixture, until well combined.

**3** Finally fold through the chocolate chips. Place tablespoons of the cookie mixture onto several baking sheets, making sure that they are spaced well apart as they will spread while cooking.

**4** Bake the cookies in the middle of the oven for 13–15 mins, until they are lightly colored and just cooked. Leave the cookies to cool on the baking sheets for 5 minutes before transferring to a wire rack to cool completely. Serve with a glass of milk.

**WHAT'S THE STORY?**

The creator of the chocolate chip cookie is said to be a Mrs. Ruth Wakefield, owner of the Toll House restaurant in Massachusetts. She devised them by accident in 1930, while trying to make regular chocolate cookies. By 1936, she had published her recipe for "chocolate crunch cookies." Soon after, manufacturers were making chocolate chips specifically for baking.

## NOW TRY...

### WHITE CHIPS

Replace the milk chocolate chips with ½ cup each of **white chocolate chips** and roughly chopped **macadamia nuts**. Bake as usual.

### FESTIVE TWIST

For a seasonal treat, replace the chocolate chips with ½ cup each of roughly chopped **pistachios** and **dried cranberries**. Bake as usual.

### TRIPLE CHOCOLATE

For the ultimate chocolate treat, replace 3 tbsp of the flour with an equal amount of **unsweetened cocoa powder**. Add ½ cup each of **dark** and **white chocolate chips**, and bake as usual.

# CRANBERRY OATMEAL COOKIES

These chewy cookies are packed with fiber-filled oats and dried fruit for a healthy treat.

★ **MAKES** 16
★ **PREP TIME** 15 mins
★ **COOK TIME** 15 mins

### Ingredients
7 tbsp unsalted butter, softened
¼ cup dark brown sugar
¾ cup sugar
1 egg
½ cup all-purpose flour
¼ tsp baking powder
¼ tsp ground cinnamon
pinch of salt
½ cup oatmeal
¼ cup dried cranberries

**1** Preheat the oven to 350°F (180°C). In a large bowl, cream together the butter and sugars with an electric hand whisk, until light and fluffy, then whisk in the egg.

**2** Sift in the flour, baking powder, cinnamon, and salt, and fold to combine. Next, fold in the oatmeal and cranberries.

**3** Place heaped tablespoons of the mixture, spaced well apart, on 2 nonstick baking sheets and bake in the center of the oven for 15 minutes, until they begin to brown at the edges. The centers should remain a little chewy.

**4** Remove the cookies from the oven. Allow them to rest on their sheets for 5 minutes before transferring them to a wire rack to cool completely.

**COOK'S TIP** These are delicious to eat, while still warm, with a glass of cold milk.

**Dried cranberries** are an excellent alternative to raisins, with a sweet yet tart flavor.

# APPLE AND CINNAMON SNICKERDOODLES

Processing dried apple into a fine powder adds a sweet yet sharp flavor to the coating on these soft cake-like cookies.

★ **MAKES** 20

★ **PREP TIME** 10 mins, plus chilling

★ **COOK TIME** 10–12 mins

### Ingredients

7 tbsp unsalted butter, softened

¾ cup sugar

1 egg

½ tsp vanilla extract

1 apple, peeled and coarsely grated

1½ cups all-purpose flour

½ tsp baking powder

pinch of salt

### For the topping

2 tbsp sugar

2 tbsp apple crisps or dried apples

1½ tsp cinnamon

**1** In a large bowl, cream together the butter and sugar with an electric hand whisk until light and fluffy. Whisk in the egg and vanilla extract, then stir in the grated apple. Sift in the flour, baking powder, and salt, then fold in to combine. Cover and chill the mixture for 30 minutes. Meanwhile, make the topping. In a food processor, process the sugar, apple crisps, and cinnamon to a fine powder.

**2** Preheat the oven to 400°F (200°C). Remove the batter from the fridge. Use a small ice-cream scoop or a tablespoon measurer to form small balls, and set them aside on a plate. Roll them briefly between your palms to even out the shape. If the batter is too soft to do this, return the plate to the fridge for a further 15 minutes to chill.

**3** Now roll the snickerdoodles in the cinnamon-sugar topping, making sure that they are well covered. Flatten them slightly between your palms and place them on 2 lined baking sheets, spaced well apart. Bake in the center of the oven for 10–12 minutes, until risen and golden brown. Remove from the oven and allow them to rest on the sheets for 5 minutes before transferring them to a wire rack to cool completely.

# CINNAMON CHURROS WITH CHOCOLATE CHILI SAUCE

These cinnamon- and sugar-sprinkled Spanish snacks take minutes to make and will be devoured just as quickly.

- ★ **MAKES** 20
- ★ **PREP TIME** 10 mins, plus cooling
- ★ **COOK TIME** 15 mins

### Ingredients

2 tbsp unsalted butter
1½ cup all-purpose flour
¼ cup sugar
1 tsp baking powder
4 cups peanut or sunflower oil
1 tsp ground cinnamon

### For the chocolate chili sauce

½ cup good-quality dark chocolate, broken into pieces
¾ cup heavy cream
1 tbsp sugar
1 tbsp unsalted butter
pinch of salt
¼ tsp chili powder or cayenne pepper, to taste

**1** Measure 1 cup of boiling water into a bowl. Add the butter and stir until it melts. Sift together the flour, half the sugar, and the baking powder into a bowl. Make a well in the center and slowly pour in the hot butter liquid, beating continuously, until you have a thick paste; you may not need all the liquid. Leave the mixture to cool and rest for 5 minutes.

**2** Pour the oil into a large, heavy-based saucepan or deep-fat fryer to a depth of at least 4in (10cm) and heat it to 375°F (190°C). Test the oil as shown in the technique on p144. Keep the correct-sized saucepan lid nearby and never leave the hot oil unattended. Regulate the temperature, making sure it remains even, or the churros will burn.

**3** Place the cooled mixture into a piping bag fitted with a ¾in (2cm) star-shaped nozzle. Pipe 2¾in (7cm) lengths of the dough directly into the hot oil using a pair of scissors to snip off the ends. Do not crowd the pan, or the temperature of the oil will go down. Cook the churros for 1–2 minutes on each side, turning them when they are golden brown. When done, remove the churros from the oil with a slotted spoon and drain on paper towels. Turn off the heat.

**4** Mix the remaining sugar and the cinnamon together on a plate and toss the churros in the mixture while still hot. Leave to cool for 5–10 minutes before serving while still warm.

**5** For the chocolate chili sauce, put the chocolate, cream, sugar, and butter in a medium, heatproof bowl over a saucepan of barely simmering water (see technique for melting chocolate on p238). Heat the mixture, stirring constantly, for 3–4 minutes until the chocolate melts and the sauce amalgamates and thickens.

**6** Take the sauce off the heat and add a pinch of salt. Add the chili powder or cayenne pepper to taste, a pinch at a time, and taste as you add it. The sauce will not immediately appear hot or spicy; the right amount of spice will be reached when it leaves a slow heat in your mouth, but does not overwhelm you. Transfer to a bowl and serve immediately with freshly made churros.

# CHOCOLATE CUSTARD-FILLED DOUGHNUTS

Doughnuts are surprisingly easy to make. These are light, airy, and taste far nicer than any store-bought varieties.

★ **MAKES** 12

★ **PREP TIME** 35 mins, plus rising and proving

★ **COOK TIME** 15–20 mins

### Ingredients

⅔ cup milk

5 tbsp unsalted butter

½ tsp vanilla extract

2 tsp dried yeast

⅓ cup sugar

2 eggs, beaten

2¼ cups all-purpose flour, preferably "00" grade, plus extra for dusting

½ tsp salt

1 quart (1 liter) peanut or sunflower oil, for deep-frying, plus extra for greasing

sugar, for coating

### For the chocolate custard filling

¾ cup whole milk

2 egg yolks

¼ cup sugar

1 tsp cornstarch

½ tsp vanilla extract

⅔ cup dark chocolate, finely chopped

**1** Heat the milk, butter, and vanilla extract in a saucepan until the butter melts. Let it cool until tepid. Whisk in the yeast and a tablespoon of the sugar. Cover and leave for 10 minutes. Mix in the eggs.

**2** Sift the flour and salt into a large bowl. Stir in the remaining sugar. Make a well in the flour and add the milk mixture. Bring together to form a rough dough. Turn the dough out onto a floured surface and knead for 10 minutes until soft and pliable. Put in an oiled bowl and cover with plastic wrap. Keep it warm for 2 hours until doubled in size.

**3** On a floured surface, knock back the dough and divide it into 12 equal pieces. Roll them between your palms to form balls. Place on baking sheets, spaced well apart. Cover with plastic wrap and a dish towel. Leave in a warm place for 1–2 hours until doubled in size.

**4** In a large, heavy-based saucepan or deep-fat fryer, heat a 4in (10cm) depth of oil to 375°F (190°C), as shown in the technique on p144. Slide the doughnuts off the sheets. Do not worry if they are flatter on one side. Carefully lower 3 at a time into the hot oil, rounded-side down. Turn after 1 minute. Remove with a slotted spoon when golden brown all over. Drain on paper towels, then, while still hot, toss them in sugar. Cool before filling.

**5** For the filling, pour the milk into a saucepan over medium heat, and heat until small bubbles form on the edge and steam rises. Do not allow the milk to boil. Using an electric mixer, whisk the egg yolks, sugar, and cornstarch together until pale yellow and thick. Slowly whisk in the warm milk. Return the mixture to the saucepan and simmer, stirring continuously, over very low heat until the sauce thickens and coats the back of a spoon. Stir in the vanilla extract, then add the chocolate and stir until it has completely melted. Remove from the heat and pour into a pitcher or bowl. Let the filling cool completely, then pour into a piping bag with a thin nozzle.

**6** Pierce each doughnut on the side and insert the nozzle. Gently squirt in about a tablespoon of the filling, until it almost starts to spill out again. Dust the hole with a little more sugar, and serve.

# BANANA AND BUTTERSCOTCH MUFFINS

Make double quantities of the butterscotch sauce as it stores well in the fridge. Gently reheat it to pour over ice cream.

★ **MAKES** 12
★ **PREP TIME** 30 mins
★ **COOK TIME** 20 mins

**Ingredients**
1¾ cups self-rising flour
⅓ cup sugar
1 tsp baking powder
pinch of fine salt
¼ cup whole milk
¼ cup peanut or sunflower oil
½ tsp vanilla extract
1 egg
2 bananas

**For the butterscotch**
4 tbsp unsalted butter
⅔ cup dark brown sugar
⅔ cup heavy cream
½ tsp vanilla extract
pinch of salt

**For the streusel topping**
¼ cup light brown sugar
½ cup all-purpose flour
2 tbsp unsalted butter, softened
½ tsp ground cinnamon

**1** First, make the butterscotch. Melt the butter in a small, heavy-based saucepan, then mix in the sugar and cook over low heat until it is no longer granular. Add the cream, vanilla extract, and salt and whisk well to combine. Bring to a boil, reduce to a low simmer, and cook, stirring constantly, for 5 minutes until thickened. Remove from the heat and pour into a large, shallow bowl to cool quicker.

**2** Meanwhile, make the streusel topping. In a small bowl or the bowl of a food processor, rub together, or pulse, all the ingredients until they resemble coarse breadcrumbs.

**3** Preheat the oven to 400°F (200°C). Sift the flour, sugar, baking powder, and salt into a large bowl. Using a hand-held blender, process the milk, oil, vanilla extract, egg, 1 banana, and three-quarters (about ⅔ cup) of the cooled butterscotch until smooth. Cut the remaining banana into small cubes.

**4** Make a well in the center of the flour mixture and mix in the liquid ingredients along with the chopped banana, being careful not to over-mix the batter.

**5** Line a muffin pan with paper liners and fill each one two-thirds full with the muffin mixture. Heat the remaining butterscotch until it is runny and divide it over the surface of each muffin. You may need to do this in 2 batches.

**6** Top each muffin with a heaped teaspoon of the streusel topping, making sure that the butterscotch is completely covered. Bake for 20 minutes until well risen, and when a toothpick inserted into the center of a muffin comes out clean. Remove the muffins from the oven and allow them to cool on a wire rack.

**COOK'S TIP** The butterscotch can be made up to 3 days ahead and stored in the fridge until needed. Any leftover streusel topping can be stored in an airtight container in the freezer and used straight from the freezer for other recipes.

# SOUTHERN-STYLE CORNBREAD

This simple bread is quick to make, and best eaten while still warm from the oven.

- ★ **SERVES** 8
- ★ **PREP TIME** 15 mins
- ★ **COOK TIME** 25–30 mins

### Ingredients

1¼ cup all-purpose flour

1¼ cup cornmeal or fine polenta

2 tsp baking powder

1 tsp salt

pinch of sugar

1¼ cup buttermilk (or to make your own, see p12)

1 egg, beaten

¼ cup vegetable oil

butter, to serve, plus extra for greasing

**1** Preheat the oven to 425°F (220°C). In a bowl, mix together the flour, cornmeal, baking powder, salt, and sugar. Stir in the buttermilk, egg, and oil, and mix until well incorporated.

**2** Pour the batter into a greased 8in (20cm) round pan, spreading it evenly.

**3** Bake in the oven for 25–30 minutes, or until golden brown. Allow to cool slightly and serve warm with butter as a side dish with soups or stews.

## SERVE WITH

### CAJUN ANDOUILLE GUMBO
SEE PAGE 112

### THREE BEAN CHILI
SEE PAGE 120

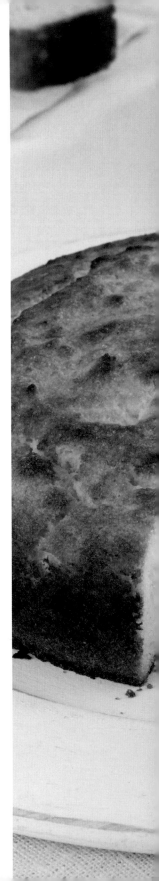

## NOW TRY...

### MUFFINS

Pour the batter into a greased 12-hole muffin pan to make individual **cornbread muffins** and bake for 25 minutes.

### CHEESE & CHILI

For a spicy twist, mix in 1 cup grated sharp **Cheddar cheese** and 1 finely chopped **jalapeño** or other mild green chile.

### BACON

Heat a greased cast-iron frying pan in the oven for 15 minutes. Remove from the oven, pour in the batter, and top with 6 **smoked bacon slices**, cut into small pieces. Return to the oven for 25 minutes.

# CAYENNE CHEDDAR CHEESE STRAWS

These crisp, crumbly canapés are particularly delicious when served still warm from the oven.

★ **MAKES** 50-60
★ **PREP TIME** 20 mins, plus chilling
★ **COOK TIME** 5-10 mins

### Ingredients
2 cups all-purpose flour, plus extra for dusting
1 tsp cayenne pepper
½ tsp smoked paprika or ancho chile powder
1 tsp salt
1 stick (8 tbsps) butter, cut into cubes
2 cups Cheddar cheese, cut into cubes
½ cup grated Parmesan cheese

**1** Put the flour, cayenne pepper, paprika, and salt in a food processor and pulse-blend. Mix in the butter and cheeses, one half at a time.

**2** Blend on high speed for 2–3 minutes, or until a soft dough forms. Wrap in plastic wrap and chill for 1 hour.

**3** Preheat the oven to 375°F (190°C). Roll out the dough to a ½in (1cm) thick rectangle, as shown in the technique below. Cut into 7in (18cm) long and ½in (1cm) wide strips. Transfer the strips onto a baking sheet lined with parchment paper. Bake for 5–10 minutes, or until crisp.

## ROLLING DOUGH

**1 Remove the plastic wrap**, turn out the dough onto a floured surface, and pat it down with your hands.

**2 Using a rolling pin**, roll out the dough evenly to a ½in (1cm) thick rectangle of the desired size.

# WHITE CHOCOLATE AND COCONUT POPCORN BALLS

Children love to help with these easy-to-make sweet treats. Roll them in colored sprinkles for added sparkle.

★ **MAKES** 10
★ **PREP TIME** 20 mins
★ **COOK TIME** 5 mins, plus drying

## Ingredients

2 tbsp peanut or sunflower oil
5 cups popcorn or popcorn kernels
2 tbsp unsalted butter, plus extra for greasing
½ cup mini marshmallows
½ cup white chocolate chips
2 tbsp shredded coconut, unsweetened

**1** If you are making the popcorn, heat the oil over high heat in a large, heavy-based saucepan. Add the popcorn kernels and shake the pan so they spread out into an even layer. Cover the pan and wait for 1–2 minutes until the corn starts popping. Reduce the heat to low and continue to cook, shaking the pan occasionally, until the popping noises have stopped. Transfer the popcorn to a large bowl to cool.

**2** Melt the butter over low heat in a small, heavy-based saucepan. Add the mini marshmallows and continue to cook over low heat for 2–3 minutes, stirring constantly, until they have just melted to a thick, sticky liquid.

**3** Pour the melted marshmallows over the popcorn and mix well. It should start to stick together. Add the chocolate chips and coconut and mix well to combine.

**4** Lightly grease your hands with a little butter and take a handful of the mixture. Compress it between your palms to make a round, compacted ball of popcorn and place on a baking sheet to dry. Repeat until you have 10 balls. Let them dry for at least 1 hour before storing in an airtight container.

**Popcorn** is simple to make, only takes a few minutes, and costs very little.

# CHILE GINGER CANDIED PECANS

A bag of candied pecans makes a lovely festive gift, prettily wrapped and hand-labeled.

★ **MAKES** 8oz (225g)
★ **PREP TIME** 10 mins
★ **COOK TIME** 20 mins

**Ingredients**
2 egg whites
1 tsp vanilla extract
½ cup light brown sugar
large pinch of chili powder
1 tbsp ground ginger
8oz (225g) whole pecans

**1** Preheat the oven to 350°F (180°C). In a small bowl, whisk the egg whites until white, soft peaks form. Stir in the vanilla extract.

**2** In a separate bowl, mix together the sugar and spices. Toss the pecans in the egg white mixture and then in the dry ingredients. Spread them out on a baking sheet lined with parchment paper. Bake for 20 minutes, or until crisp.

**3** Remove the pecans from the oven and toss in the spice mixture again. Leave to cool. Serve as a snack or as a topping in salads, soups, or ice cream.

# GOOEY S'MORES BARS

These s'mores bars, with a cinnamon-flavored ganache, are an easy-to-make alternative to the traditional camping treat.

★ **MAKES** 12

★ **PREP TIME** 15 mins

★ **COOK TIME** 40 mins, plus chilling

## Ingredients

1 stick (8 tbsps) butter, melted, plus extra for greasing

½ cup light brown sugar

½ cup sugar

4 eggs

1 tsp vanilla extract

6 graham crackers

½ cup all-purpose flour

1 tsp baking powder

11oz bag mini marshmallows, for the topping

## For the ganache

1 cup semisweet chocolate, broken into small pieces

1 tsp ground cinnamon

½ cup heavy cream

**1** Preheat the oven to 350°F (180°C). Grease and line a 9in (23cm) square baking pan.

**2** Using an electric hand whisk, cream the butter and the sugars in a bowl. Add the eggs, one at a time, and the vanilla extract and whisk until light and fluffy.

**3** In a food processor, process the graham crackers until they resemble breadcrumbs. Alternatively, place the crackers in a plastic food bag and crush with a rolling pin. Pour into a large bowl and add the flour, baking powder, and egg mixture. Stir to combine. Pour the batter into the baking pan and bake for 35 minutes, or until golden brown.

**4** For the ganache, place the chocolate, cinnamon, and cream in a small heatproof bowl over a saucepan of simmering water (see technique for melting chocolate on p238). The bowl should not touch the water. Stir occasionally until the chocolate melts. Remove immediately.

**5** Pour the ganache over the cracker base and top with the marshmallows. Broil on very low heat, until toasted and melted. Let it cool for 15 minutes before transferring to the fridge. Chill for 30–45 minutes; this will make it easier to slice. Cut into equal-sized bars and serve at room temperature.

# CHOCOLATE MARSHMALLOW FUDGE

This recipe is ideal for children to make. It is quick, easy, and ready in the time it takes for the chocolate to set.

- ★ **MAKES** 36 squares
- ★ **PREP TIME** 5 mins
- ★ **COOK TIME** 5 mins, plus cooling

### Ingredients

9oz bag mini marshmallows

3 cups semisweet or dark chocolate

16oz (450g) can condensed milk

¼ cup whole milk

1 tsp vanilla extract

**1** Line a 9in (23cm) square baking sheet with parchment paper. Lay out the marshmallows on the tray. In a saucepan, heat the chocolate, condensed milk, and milk over medium heat. Cook, stirring frequently, until the chocolate melts and all the ingredients are combined.

**2** Remove from the heat, add the vanilla extract, and stir to combine. Spread the chocolate mixture over the marshmallows and set aside to cool completely. When the fudge has set, cut into 1½in (4cm) squares and serve.

**Marshmallows** don't just belong by the campfire—try using them in the kitchen as well.

# PEAR AND CARDAMOM BUTTER

The complex flavors of pears and cardamom are an exciting twist on the more usual apple butter.

- ★ **MAKES** 2 x 10fl oz (300ml) jars
- ★ **PREP TIME** 15 mins
- ★ **COOK TIME** 1 hr, plus cooling

## Ingredients

4 pears, about 14oz (400g) in total
¾ cup apple cider vinegar
½ cup light brown sugar
½ tbsp cardamom pods, ground
pinch of salt

**1** Core and peel the pears, as shown in the technique below, then roughly chop. In a saucepan, combine the pears, vinegar, ½ cup of water, sugar, cardamom, and salt. Bring to a boil on high heat, then reduce the heat and simmer, uncovered, for 1 hour, or until the pears are tender. Remove from the heat and allow to cool completely for about 1 hour.

**2** Blend in a food processor, or purée with a hand-held blender. Spread generously on toast and serve with hot coffee.

**COOK'S TIP** The spread will keep for up to 2 weeks in an airtight container.

## CORING AND PEELING A PEAR

1 **Use a melon baller** or a teaspoon to scoop out the small core in the base of the pear.

2 **Use a vegetable peeler** or a small, sharp knife to pare off the skin thinly and evenly, then remove the stalk.

# LAVENDER CHOCOLATE PRETZEL RODS

A small amount of lavender adds a delicate fragrance and subtle flavor to these sophisticated snacks.

★ **MAKES** 20

★ **PREP TIME** 10 mins

★ **COOK TIME** 10 mins, plus drying

### Ingredients

5½oz (150g) dark chocolate chips or squares

20 large, thick pretzel rods or knotted pretzels

3 tbsp dried culinary lavender

**1** Melt the chocolate in a small heatproof bowl over a saucepan of simmering water, as shown in the technique below.

**2** Dip two-thirds of a pretzel rod or knotted pretzel into the melted chocolate, tilting the bowl for a good coating. Carefully drip off any excess chocolate into the bowl. Continue to dip all the pretzel rods.

**3** Sprinkle over the lavender sparingly and transfer the pretzel rods to a lined baking sheet to dry. You can also try topping the pretzel rods with sprinkles, crushed nuts, dried fruit, or candy pieces for a delicious alternative.

## MELTING CHOCOLATE

**1 Put the chocolate** in a small heatproof bowl over a saucepan of simmering water, making sure the bowl does not touch the water.

**2 Stir occasionally** with a metal spoon and remove the bowl from the saucepan as soon as the chocolate has melted.

# PISTACHIO BRITTLE

Brittles are simple to make, and you can try combining different dried fruit and nuts to find your favorite combination.

- ★ **SERVES** 6-8
- ★ **PREP TIME** 5 mins
- ★ **COOK TIME** 18 mins, plus cooling

### Ingredients

1 cup sugar

½ cup light corn syrup

1 cup shelled pistachios

2 tbsp butter, cut into cubes, plus extra for greasing

1 tsp baking soda

1 tsp vanilla extract

**1** In a heavy-based saucepan, combine the sugar, corn syrup, and ¼ cup water over medium heat. Cook, stirring frequently with a wooden spoon, as shown in the technique below.

**2** At this hard breaking point, add the pistachios. Continue stirring until the temperature rises to 325°F (160°C) again.

**3** Remove from the heat and stir in the butter, baking soda, and vanilla extract. Continue to stir as it foams and the butter melts.

**4** Pour onto a greased 9 x 14in (23 x 35cm) baking sheet and let it cool completely. Break into pieces and store in an airtight container.

**COOK'S TIP** If you do not have a sugar thermometer, drop a small amount of the mixture into a glass of cold water, and if the candy breaks, it is hot enough.

## BOILING SUGAR

**1 In a heavy-based saucepan**, heat the sugar, corn syrup, and ¼ cup water over medium heat.

**2 Cook, stirring frequently**, until a sugar thermometer dipped into the liquid reads 325°F (160°C) and the sugar turns brittle and golden brown.

# FRESH BERRY COMPOTE WITH VANILLA AND THYME

Cook down ripe summer berries to make this sweet, syrupy compote, perfect for serving with pancakes or ice cream.

★ **SERVES** 4
★ **PREP TIME** 10 mins
★ **COOK TIME** 20 mins

**Ingredients**
½ cup sugar
1 vanilla pod, split and
   seeds scraped
sprig of thyme
5½oz (150g) blackberries
3½oz (100g) dark cherries,
   pitted and halved weight (see
   technique, below)
3½oz (100g) blueberries

**1** Put the sugar, vanilla pod, thyme, and 2 tbsp water in a medium, heavy-based saucepan, stir together, and bring to a boil. Add the blackberries and cherries, reduce the heat and simmer, covered, for 8–10 minutes, until the berries start to break down and release their juices.

**2** Remove the lid, add the blueberries, increase the heat, and continue to cook the compote for a further 8–10 minutes, stirring occasionally, until the sauce has thickened and reduced, and the berries are soft.

**3** Remove from the heat and cool. Remove the vanilla pod and thyme before serving cold, or at room temperature.

**COOK'S TIP** This deliciously dark compote will keep for several days in the fridge, and is marvelous over ice cream, yogurt, or Homemade granola (see p60) for a morning treat.

## PITTING CHERRIES

**To remove pits with a pitter**, place the cherry in the pitter, stem-side down, and press until the pit emerges from the hole at the bottom.

**If using a knife**, slice the cherry lengthwise in two, cutting all the way around the pit. Twist and separate the halves and remove the pit.

# NO-COOK SPICY SUMMER RELISH

This fresh, vibrant relish takes seconds to make and is great in burgers, with hot dogs, or even in wraps and sandwiches.

★ **SERVES** 6-8

★ **PREP TIME** 10 mins

**Ingredients**

1 red bell pepper
1 yellow bell pepper
1 small red onion, roughly
    chopped
1 garlic clove
½ jalapeño or other mild green
    chile, seeded
3 tbsp rice wine vinegar
    or white vinegar
2 tsp sugar
salt and freshly ground
    black pepper
good-quality mayonnaise,
    to serve (optional)

 Seed and roughly chop the red and yellow peppers, as shown in the technique below. In a food processor, pulse the bell peppers, onion, garlic, and jalapeño until finely chopped.

 Put the chopped vegetables in a nonreactive (not aluminum or cast-iron) bowl. Add the vinegar, sugar, and season well. Stir until well combined, then cover and chill for at least 4 hours.

**3** To serve, drain off any excess liquid and serve as it is or stir in some mayonnaise for a creamier finish.

**COOK'S TIP** This relish will keep in the fridge for up to 5 days, tightly sealed.

## PREPARING A PEPPER

**1 Place it on its side** and cut off the top and bottom. Stand on one of the cut ends and slice in half lengthwise. Remove the core and seeds.

**2 Lay each section flat** on the cutting board. Remove the remaining pale, fleshy ribs, then roughly cut the flesh into chunks.

# QUICK STOVETOP SAUERKRAUT

Traditionally, sauerkraut is fermented over several weeks. Try this almost instant version for a quick, easy alternative.

★ **SERVES** 4
★ **PREP TIME** 10 mins
★ **COOK TIME** 1½ hrs

## Ingredients

1 tbsp olive oil
2 garlic cloves, crushed
1 small white onion, diced
1 head of green cabbage, shredded
2 cups (500ml) apple cider vinegar
2 tbsp salt
1 tbsp caraway seeds

**1** Heat the oil in a deep, straight-sided frying pan or Dutch oven. Add the garlic to the pan and cook over medium heat until golden. Stir in the onion and cook for 10 minutes, or until translucent.

**2** Add the cabbage to the pan along with ½ cup of water, the vinegar, salt, and caraway seeds. Bring to a boil, reduce to a simmer, cover, and cook over a low heat for 1½ hours. Serve warm with hot dogs or sausages.

**COOK'S TIP** This sauerkraut is also great added to soups and stews for a healthy, warming meal.

**Shredded cabbage**, cooked in this way, will keep for several weeks in the fridge.

# SPICY CHOW CHOW

This simple refrigerator pickle is like a spicy pickled coleslaw. It is delicious with cold meats and cheeses, as well as in sandwiches and wraps.

- ★ **MAKES** 4 x 10fl oz (300ml) jars
- ★ **PREP TIME** 20 mins
- ★ **COOK TIME** 10 mins

**For the slaw**

5 green tomatoes, finely chopped
1 green bell pepper, seeded and finely chopped
1 red bell pepper, seeded and finely chopped
1 red onion, finely chopped
3 garlic cloves, crushed
½ head of green cabbage, shredded
1 tbsp sea salt

**For the pickle**

2½ cups white vinegar
1 cup light brown sugar
1 tbsp mustard seeds
1 tsp celery seeds
1 tsp chili flakes
3 tbsp sea salt

**1** To make the slaw, combine the vegetables with the sea salt in a large bowl and mix well. Cover and chill in the fridge overnight.

**2** Drain the vegetables and transfer them to a medium saucepan. Add the vinegar, sugar, mustard seeds, celery seeds, chili flakes, and the sea salt. Simmer the vegetable mixture over medium heat for 15 minutes.

**3** Divide the mixture between 4 clean, sterilized jars. (To sterilize the jars, see step 1, p249.) The relish will keep for up to 2 weeks in the fridge.

## SERVE WITH

**BREAKFAST BURRITOS**
SEE PAGE 68

**SHRIMP AND GRITS**
SEE PAGE 110

# HOT PEPPER JELLY

## This simple jelly is an easy introduction to preserving, without the need for traditional water-bath canning.

★ **MAKES** 4 x 10fl oz
(300ml) jars

★ **PREP TIME** 20 mins

★ **COOK TIME** 10 mins

### Ingredients

14oz (400g) jalapeños or
other mild green chiles,
finely chopped

3½oz (100g) green bell
peppers, seeded and roughly
chopped

2 tbsp pectin

1½ cups white vinegar

2 cups honey

**1** Process the jalapeños and peppers in a food processor to make a purée. Transfer the purée to a saucepan and combine with the pectin, vinegar, and honey. Bring to a boil, then reduce the heat and let it simmer for 10 minutes.

**2** Pour into 4 clean, sterilized jars and tightly screw on the lids. (To sterilize the jars, see step 1, opposite.) Leave to set for 1 hour before serving. The jelly will keep for up to 2 weeks in the fridge.

**Green bell pepper**
lends a mild, sweet
flavor to this jelly.

# REFRIGERATOR PICKLES

There is nothing quite like the crunch of homemade refrigerator pickles, which are fresher than store-bought equivalents.

★ **MAKES** 2 x 7fl oz (200ml) jars
★ **PREP TIME** 10 mins

### Ingredients

¼ cup sugar
2 tsp salt
¾ cup white wine vinegar or
   rice wine vinegar
freshly ground black pepper
4-5 small pickling cucumbers,
   thinly sliced
1 tbsp finely chopped
   dill fronds
½ tsp dill seeds, lightly crushed

**1** Preheat the oven to 275°F (140°C). To sterilize the jars, wash them thoroughly and place them upside-down on a baking sheet. Put them in the oven for at least 15 minutes. Put the lids in a metal bowl and pour over a few cups of boiling water. Leave for 5 minutes, then remove and leave to drain. Dry well with paper towels.

**2** Put the sugar and salt in a bowl and add a little of the vinegar. Whisk until the salt and sugar dissolve, then add the remaining vinegar and a good grinding of pepper.

**3** Once the jars are cold, layer the cucumbers in the jars, adding a sprinkling of chopped dill and a few dill seeds between each layer.

**4** When the jars are full, pour over the vinegar mixture and seal. Shake the jars to disperse the liquid evenly and refrigerate overnight for them to get really crispy.

**COOK'S TIP** These pickles will keep in the fridge for up to 1 month, packed in a sterilized, sealed jar. Make sure they are always covered with vinegar.

Step-by-step preparation techniques are in *italic*.

## ACKNOWLEDGMENTS

**Caroline Bretherton would like to thank:** Borra Garson and all at Deborah McKenna for their work on my behalf; Peggy Vance, Dawn Henderson, Bob Bridle, and all at DK for their enthusiasm and encouragement; and Elena Rosemond-Hoerr for being such a fabulous co-author and photographer.

**Elena Rosemond-Hoerr would like to thank:** my sweet husband Dan for his impeccable taste-testing skills; my incredible co-author Caroline for holding my hand through the cookbook writing process; and Bob Bridle and the patient team at DK for their support and enthusiasm.

**DK would like to thank:** Stuart West and Elena Rosemond-Hoerr for photography; Penny Stock and Lisa Pettibone for photography art direction; Jane Lawrie for food styling; Wei Tang for prop styling; Jane Bamforth, Anna Burges-Lumsden, Sue Davie, Jan Fullwood, Chris Gates, Katy Greenwood, Anne Harnan, and Sue Harris for recipe testing; Corinne Masciocchi for proofreading; and Marie Lorimer for the index.

## PICTURE CREDITS